IT DOESN'T TAKE A GENIUS

FIVE TRUTHS TO INSPIRE SUCCESS IN EVERY STUDENT

**RANDALL McCUTCHEON
AND TOMMIE LINDSEY**

McGraw-Hill

New York   Chicago   San Francisco   Lisbon   London   Madrid   Mexico City
Milan   New Delhi   San Juan   Seoul   Singapore   Sydney   Toronto

LB
1062
.6
.M43
2006

The *McGraw·Hill* Companies

Library of Congress Cataloging-in-Publication Data

McCutcheon, Randall, 1949–
    It doesn't take a genius : five truths to inspire success in every student / by Randall McCutcheon, Tommie Lindsey.
        p.   cm.
    ISBN 0-07-146084-5
    1. Academic achievement—United States—Case studies.   2. School improvement programs—United States—Case studies.   3. Education, Secondary—Aims and objectives—United States—Case studies.   4. Educational leadership—United States—Case studies.   I. Lindsey, Tommie.   II. Title.

    LB1062.6.M43   2005
    371.1—dc22   2005053131

1 2 3 4 5 6 7 8 9 0   FGR/FGR   0 9 8 7 6 5

ISBN 0-07-146084-5

Interior design by Pamela Juárez
Interior illustrations by Sidney Harris

McGraw-Hill books are available at special quantity discounts to use as premiums and sales promotions, or for use in corporate training programs. For more information, please write to the Director of Special Sales, Professional Publishing, McGraw-Hill, Two Penn Plaza, New York, NY 10121-2298. Or contact your local bookstore.

This book is printed on acid-free paper.

CONTENTS

FOREWORD

Randall McCutcheon and Tommie Lindsey have captured in this book the essence of what I choose to call the sacred privilege of teaching—what it means to be blessed with the extraordinary opportunity of helping shape young lives.

These two inspiring and innovative teachers are much like my own mentor, a man named Charlie, whom I first met fifty years ago at a wonderful Jesuit high school in Brooklyn. Charlie simultaneously taught us history, literature, art, and music—and he was master of all of them. For three years, for an hour each day, five days a week, he led us from the cave paintings of Altamira and the sounds of simple percussion to Jackson Pollock and Aaron Copland. To him, the word *boundary* had no meaning. After the Jesuits followed the heinous example of Walter O'Malley and pulled out of Brooklyn (closing the high school where he taught), Charlie taught for several years at a yeshiva, and, until he turned eighty-four, he volunteered at Mother Teresa's hospice for AIDS patients.

Because of Charlie, I embraced teaching even as I moved from high school to college. In 1960, as a seventeen-year-old college sophomore, I began the daily trip from the Bronx to St. Brendan's High School in Brooklyn, where I would invest nearly eighty hours a week for the next fifteen years. The school has been closed now for more than twenty-five years, but you will recognize the girls.

They were the daughters of police officers, firefighters, and sanitation workers. At the time, the hopes of these young women generally did not include much beyond the world they knew—indeed, for some, a trip to Manhattan (let alone to a museum or concert in what they called the City) was beyond imagination. They were expected to be home after school to help clean the house and care for siblings. Most were not expected to go to college.

I was too young and naive to notice these limitations. High school debate and Charlie had opened the world of ideas and experiences to me, and I had thrived. So also, I concluded, would the girls. As a result, for fifteen years (and for all those hours each week, including the road trips), using a debate team as the linchpin, I did with the girls what Charlie had done with me: sharing the great books, art, music, the museums of New York, and the mountains or canyons of any state to which we could drive. We lived his mantra: in living, reach for the new experience; always try to play another octave of the piano.

And the girls responded. Not only did they dominate high school debate for fifteen years, but each of them went to college on a scholarship. In the process, I was captured for the fulfilling life of teaching, and I was taught that the single most important thing in teaching is to set high expectations for the students or, as our authors explain, be the first believer. As Charlie put it, "Students don't fail; teachers fail."

These lessons animate my life today—for, even as NYU's president, I continue to teach, just as I did during my fourteen years as dean of the NYU School of Law. This year I have taught two courses: a freshman seminar on the Supreme Court and religion and a course for juniors and seniors called Baseball as a Road to God. Next year I'll teach three, as I return to teaching in the School of Law. Friends ask how I can teach that many courses and do all that I do; I ask how could I do what I do if I did not teach.

The gratitude for Randy and Tommie that their students have expressed in these pages echo my own for Charlie, and while sadly he is no longer with us, whenever I try to play another octave, I hear his great, booming voice of encouragement ringing in my ears.

—*Dr. John Sexton, President, New York University*

Acknowledgments

First, I'd like to thank God for creating a "way out of no way." Thanks to my grandmother for maintaining the family structure in my life, Lois for guiding and rearing two wonderful children, Erika and Terence for loving me in spite of my shortcomings, Mrs. Dukes for fifty-three years of friendship and stability, all of my students for making my teaching career the experience of a lifetime, all of my friends for their support, and all of the teachers who make the day-to-day sacrifices that give me my inspiration.

A special thanks to all of my fellow forensics coaches (especially Tim, Jay, Steve, and Reed) for their time, energy, and creativity; Mike for his unselfishness and hard work in helping with this book; and, of course, Randy for making this dream come true. Lastly, thanks and gratitude to Terri DeBono and Steve Rosen (producers of *Accidental Hero: Room 408*) for stepping out on faith.

—*Tommie Lindsey*

This book is for my grandmother, my first teacher.

I would also like to express my deepest appreciation to Jane Durso for her perfect wisdom and pen wielding; my students, who contributed not only to this book but to the teacher I became; William Moss, Darwin Salestrom, and Robert Bovinette, who helped me be me; and Bob Marks and the other coaches who taught me along the way.

And a special "Standing O" for Tommie, the inspiration for this book.

—*Randall McCutcheon*

PREFACE

Soap and education are not as sudden as a massacre,
but they are more deadly in the long run.

—*Mark Twain*

Twain's cynicism notwithstanding, we all want to be the ones who survive the massacre. We all want the Answer. In a cartoon that appeared in *Phi Delta Kappan*, it was apparent from the faces in the drawing that a highly distressed teacher had just asked a librarian for help. The librarian's response was the caption: "You'll find 'Teaching Methods That Never Fail' under fiction."

If you find yourself nodding in agreement, read on. Pierre Clark, one of Tommie Lindsey's students, suggested the title for this book. In the award-winning PBS documentary *Accidental Hero: Room 408*, Pierre, a ninth grader at the time, was asked why he quit the football team to join Tommie's forensics team. Pierre replied, "I saw how many forensics kids were going to college, which was about 100 percent, and I saw how many football players were going to college, which was about 15 percent. You don't have to be a genius to figure that out."

Maybe Pierre is wrong. Maybe you do have to be a genius to figure that out. What are the ways to inspire most students to succeed? How do you find those "teaching methods that never fail"? No one would dispute that millions of students are uninspired. Not much new there. Nearly fifty years ago, John F. Kennedy warned, "A child miseducated is a child lost." Clearly, we have lost far too many children since then.

So how do we find this genius who can save the children? I read that when Coach Bill Belichick took his New England Patriots to the Super Bowl, major newspapers called him a genius 609 times. In his entire life, Albert Einstein was described by those same newspapers as a genius only 486 times. Cultural relativity, it seems, is not a theory but a fact.

Tommie and I don't pretend to be geniuses, but we have figured a few things out during our decades of standing in front of classrooms. The most important thing we have learned is that there are no simple answers. That doesn't mean, as the *Phi Delta Kappan* cartoon implies, a teacher is doomed to fail. We realize that a teacher changes the lives of children one child at a time. We believe the five truths we share in this book have helped us to change countless lives for the better.

If you read between the lines, you will find out something about us. Tommie and I believe that all children are gifted and, at the same time, at risk. Although we both became members of the National Forensic League (an organization that has had more than a million student members), we are not writing about coaching speech. True, you will find numerous references to what we learned as coaches. But the truths we share are universal. Coaches are teachers. Or they should be. We truly hope that teachers, parents, and students will be inspired by what they read in these pages.

You will soon discover that we have included the thoughts of many of our students. Some of the students engage in truth talking (as opposed to trash talking), and others describe an epiphany

" 'C' IN ASTROPHYSICS, 'B MINUS' IN CALCULUS...
WHAT KIND OF GENIUS ARE YOU?"

they experienced during their education in "When They Get It." The "Practical Matters" you encounter throughout the book are an invention of mine for parents and teachers who want to challenge students in constructive and creative ways.

A final thought. I wish that you could have met Tommie the way I did: through the members of his Logan High School speech team. In the early 1990s, I was an instructor at a summer speech camp held at the University of California, Berkeley. Some of Tommie's students attended the camp one summer. They were easily the hardest working kids at the camp. I remember that unlike the kids from other teams, Tommie's students made a point of thanking me after every coaching session. They seemed genuinely appreciative of my efforts.

As we approached the lunch break one day, I noticed Tommie's students walking by. Each student had two paper bags. I called out to them, "You kids must be mighty hungry." They explained to me that each student had packed two lunches: one to eat and one to give to a homeless person on Telegraph Avenue.

I have always thought that a team assumes the personality of its coach. And for the most part, the team members' actions reflect the values of the person who leads them. As I watched Tommie's students that day on Telegraph Avenue, I knew that something special was taking place at Logan High School. It didn't take a genius to figure that out.

—*Randall McCutcheon*

INTRODUCTION

WHY I BECAME A TEACHER

Does your job ever cause you to drift toward existentialism? Just for a brief moment, you are sitting there at work, and the thought slams into your conscience clearly and boldly: Why did I choose this profession? Why am I here? Perhaps an illustration is called for—a glimpse into my typical workday. I arrive at James Logan High School at half past the crack of dawn. I gulp down my vanilla caffe latte (with nonfat milk). I glance at the newspaper. I decipher my handwritten notes from yesterday and assemble the day's lesson and lecture plans, and then it happens again. It's suddenly eight o'clock in the morning, and my second-period students materialize in my classroom. After that, from approximately eight until three in the afternoon, chaos ensues. Sure, it's a form of controlled chaos, but it's chaos nevertheless.

Lectures, questions, meeting discussions, trying to make concepts clear, unpacking confusion; office hours, phone calls, haggling with the school administrators between periods, mountains of paperwork for tournament travel, grading, speech text proofreading; more lectures, more questions, putting out interpersonal fires between students, jotting down notes for the next day's lesson plans, telling the undiagnosed attention deficit disorder kid to sit down for the fifth time, the idea of early retirement in my aching head. If anyone tells you that teaching is an easy job—well, they haven't been in the trenches as long as I have. There are indeed times when simply quitting seems like the best option, but still, I keep on trudging. Those of us in the teaching profession realize that such fleeting episodes of doubt are merely a distraction. What we teachers know is this: if you set aside the long hours, the less-than-stellar pay, the troublemakers, and the politics, you will find the unbridled truth about the art and the practice of education staring you in the face. Teaching rewards those of us willing to pay the price. Any teacher worth his or her weight in chalk dust or dry eraser pen will tell you the same.

What other job allows you to change thousands of lives? I've had the incredible privilege of helping kids discover one of the most important mysteries of life: who they are. Identity, sense of self, and self-esteem. These three interrelated ideas can make the difference in the development of a young mind. The brain of a typical high school student is constantly growing, adapting, and learning, incorporating not just the lessons gleaned in the classroom—the reading, the writing, and the arithmetic—but also about the world and where they will fit into it. It is amazing, the transformation that takes place when you encourage students to find their identity. Not only do they begin to realize who they are, they enthusiastically take it to the next level, focusing on that newfound knowledge. They begin to map out their futures.

I became a teacher so that I could enable kids to find something within their lives that would assist them in learning their worth in society, and in life. The most poignant and powerful tool that people can use to discover their worth is their voice. Albert Einstein was right: "It is the supreme art of teaching to awaken the joy in creative expression and knowledge."

In my thirty years of teaching, I've found that the best way to reveal that creative spirit is through public speaking. I've always believed that the voice is a window on the soul. The seat of the soul is, as Gerald de Nerval suggests, "not inside or outside a person, but the very place they overlap and meet the world." I've discovered that when teenagers come into high school, they have a number of issues to confront: anger, loneliness, confusion, the fears that accompany the journey from childhood to adulthood. It is my role as a teacher to provide kids with what they need to better address the issues and barriers they will inevitably face.

I can remember the elementary school teacher who gave me my voice. I was always a vocal person, so she didn't have to help me with refining my word economy or polishing my elocution skills. No, her profound lesson did something else. In one day's work, she taught me an important truth about myself, and I've never forgotten that lesson. In school I had always felt a little inferior since I didn't have the nice, clean clothing worn by all the other kids in my class. My parents grew up poor; I had eight other brothers and sisters. As you can imagine, there just wasn't a lot of money left over for new school clothes. My teacher noticed this—not just my ripped pants, but also how my appearance affected my self-esteem as well as how I performed as a student.

That pivotal day, my teacher took me to Sears and bought me two pairs of pants and two shirts. After that single act of generosity, I had suitable clothes to wear to school. I didn't feel inferior anymore. Looking back, it seems such a small thing, such an easily forgotten detail, but the fact that my clothing was tattered was a devastating barrier to my ability to learn. Somehow my teacher knew that by having that barrier lifted, I could excel. She was right. I began to feel good about myself, and I was given another gift. My voice.

For the last thirty years, I've been doing the same thing with my students. I may not have literally taken them to Sears to buy fresh clothes and shirts, but the essence of the selfless act remains. Take away the barriers to learning, and an awakening will occur. I have seen this simple truth played out time and time again over the course of my career. If you help students remove or face the obstacles in their lives, they will soar.

Yes, there are times when the chaos gets to be too much, when the din of the classroom gets too loud, when I have ten students lined up outside my office to talk about grades, when my head is throbbing with another migraine—and I glance at the calendar and wonder why June is taking so long to come around.

But the existential questions come and go quickly because there have been so many student success stories. Even when my days are compounded with stress—the lectures, the questions, the clashing personalities, the headaches, and the drama—the success stories negate any hint of doubt. Why did I choose this profession? Why am I here? Simply put, I'm here to make a difference. It's a daunting responsibility, one I've undertaken for the last three decades. Standing at the lectern in front of my students, I know, deep in my heart and soul, that I was meant for this life. A teacher is born to teach. This responsibility is profound. No matter what a kid is wearing or what socioeconomic background he or she is from, I care because I believe in what is possible.

—*Tommie Lindsey*

THE FIRST TRUTH

BE THE FIRST BELIEVER

Be the First Believer

Randy

One needs something to believe in, something for which one can have wholehearted enthusiasm. One needs to feel that one's life has meaning, that one is needed in this world.

> —*Hannah Senesh, diarist, poet, playwright, and parachutist in the Jewish resistance under the British Armed Forces during World War II*

We begin with this truth because it is the most essential. You cannot teach effectively if you do not first believe in yourself. Moreover, you must then believe in the potential of each child. A child must feel "needed in this world." This is not as easy as it sounds. Some children will test your "belief" commitment. The daily betrayals and disappointments may make you occasionally question the meaning of your life.

Faith is fragile. But faith in each child has never been more necessary. The poet Lawrence Ferlinghetti was right: the world is not always a "beautiful place to be born into." As parents and teachers, we must change that world. One child at a time. I learned of the power in this truth long, long ago.

How I Spent My Teaching Vacation

In 1965 I was an intransigent desk-perado lost in the bewilderness of high school. Like many of my friends, I led a life of quiet indigestion. That is to say, I couldn't stomach the boredom of sophomore year.

Somebody is boring me. I think it's me. —*Dylan Thomas*

Of course, I was into a different Dylan at the time. Still, I knew that my boot heels would not be wandering anywhere soon. Then one day I found myself thumbing through the *Hastings Daily Tribune*, a newspaper from the far more cosmopolitan north country. And there was a photograph of two students holding up a trophy. They appeared to have just returned from Sunday school. And, in a way that I didn't understand at the time, they had.

The caption beneath the photo explained that the trophy was earned at a debate tournament. A what? Poring over the accompanying article, I discovered that debate was a form of organized arguing. Furthermore, you got to travel to these tournament things. Two desirable attributes for any youthful activity. You get to argue and you get to leave town. But Superior High School did not have a debate team. So I, naturally, set about to change that. What follows is apocryphal of miracles.

My first step was to enlist the help of some unsuspecting adult. I settled on Mrs. Bohling, a kindly English teacher. She was easily led to believe that she would merely have to drive us to these tournament things and that she wouldn't, in fact, have to coach us. Next, I advertised in the school's daily announcements: "Organizational Meeting for the Debate Team. Come to Mrs. Bohling's room right after school."

Amazingly, three other students showed up. Now what? So I got on the phone to Hastings High School. When they finally tracked down their debate coach, I proclaimed, "We want to debate you." He nicely let me know that the debate season was over for that year. Undeterred, I proclaimed again, "We want to debate you."

Eventually he relented. The next week we were on the road. "The dream is alive," I must have thought. Arriving at Hastings High School, we were led to the arena for the slaughter that never came. After a few seconds of awkward silence, it became apparent that we knew nothing and suspected less. Their team members bandied about words like *inherency* and *status quo*. We nodded politely. Given that we came from a rural community, one can only imagine what we thought *stock issues* were.

As we drove home that evening from Hastings, Mrs. Bohling must have believed, "Well, that's that." She was not that lucky. The next fall I asked the Hastings' debate coach to mail us a schedule of those tournament things. On the road again. This time we journeyed to the state capital and our first actual competition. I remembered from the photo in the newspaper that debate competitors must look presentable. Fortunately, I had a red blazer, green jeans, and Day-Glo red socks. The blazer and jeans, however, were two sizes too small. Picture an emaciated Santa—experiencing an unexpected growth spurt—on casual Friday. Some of my opponents probably thought the carnival had come to town.

At the tournament site, I noticed that teams had to switch sides after each round. Initially, I was horrified by the realization that I would have to defend both the affirmative and negative sides of the issue. Especially given that I didn't understand either side.

The topic that year had to do with compulsory arbitration of labor-management disputes. Not much there for a farm kid to warm up to. Then it came to me. All we had to do was write down everything our opponents said in the first round and then use those same arguments in the second round when we switched sides. And repeat that process over and over. The cumulative effect: the other teams and their coaches would teach us what we needed to know.

For three tournaments, we studied under the tutelage of very willing opponents. We lost eleven consecutive rounds. Saying "we lost" is generous. We were hammered by far superior teams. But we didn't care. We understood that they were better coached and had worked harder. They deserved to win. By the fourth trip into battle, we were finally armed with arguments and ready to reason. As the sun set on our fourth tournament thing, we were holding up a trophy.

Admittedly, we had fathomed enough about debate strategy from our opponents to occasionally defeat them with their own arguments. But something more important was at play here. After each humbling loss, we never gave up on ourselves. We never quit. And that was the real beginning of my teaching vacation, when I learned an essential truth: *you* must be the first believer.

A NUT WITH A MISSION

Tommie

The minute you settle for less than you deserve,
you get even less than you settled for.

—*Maureen Dowd*

I've always had such respect and appreciation for Marva Collins. Collins is a teacher who never "settled." Her dedication to young people led her to start Westside Preparatory School in her own home in 1975. Using two of her bedrooms for classrooms, Collins took in students who had dropped out of school in discouragement, had been expelled from public schools, or were simply failing because they were labeled "incorrigible" or "unteachable." She went the extra mile for her students, and many, if not all, of her students have attended college. What's her secret? There was nothing miraculous or magical about her students' success. It took love and determination.

Thirty years of teaching have taught me that it takes not only love and determination but also belief to reach all students. Case in point: a student I taught several years ago was rejected by UCLA, one of the top universities in the country. He was told that his 3.3 grade point average and SAT score of 1100 were not as competitive as scores of the students who had already been accepted into the university. Still, there was something within this student that I could see, though the admissions committee could not see it yet—a determination, a self-respect, and a dignity that was unlike any other student I've taught. I knew, for example, that his mother had had to go into the hospital for major surgery. Since she was a single parent, it was difficult for her to make arrangements for someone to care for her after her surgery, but this student took care of his mother until she was able to get back on her feet. Having witnessed his caring nature and having watched him compete on the forensics team, I was certain that this kid was destined to be successful in whatever university he chose.

TERRY FLENNAUGH
LOGAN HIGH SCHOOL

I wonder how many people told Lindsey he was crazy for trying to get me into UCLA. Or how many people told him that it was impossible for him to get a kid with no AP or honors courses and a GPA of 3.3 into a tier-one research university like UCLA. All I know is that my life has been forever changed because of his determination and relentlessness. Mr. Lindsey was the first teacher in my twelve years of education who ever talked to me about going to college. He was able to see something in me that other teachers had overlooked. He pushed me to greatness in competitive speech and debate as well as in the way I carried myself as a young man. So when the time came to apply to schools, Mr. Lindsey was instrumental in getting me to apply to UCLA. Through the entire process, I kept telling myself that I was doing this because Lindsey had invested so much time and energy in me, but I never felt like I had a fighting chance at getting into UCLA.

When the first rejection letter came, I wasn't surprised, but I was worried that Lindsey would take it hard. He, however, was unfazed and immediately got on the phone with the admissions office at UCLA to find out about the appeal process. Rejection letter after rejection letter, Lindsey remained determined to get me into UCLA; even after I personally had given up what little hope I initially had. All the time, I would be doing makeup work to increase my GPA, meeting with UCLA representatives in meetings that Lindsey had set up, or reworking appeals letters, all for Lindsey. I felt that it was the least I could do for all the work he had put into this process. Three appeals later and two months after other students had been admitted into UCLA, I received a call from my mother telling me that UCLA had left a message saying that I had finally been admitted into their university. When I gave Lindsey the news, he was so happy he couldn't stop smiling. I'll never forget what Lindsey did for me and the fight he put up for me against seemingly impossible odds. Call him a nut—I'll call him my hero.

Another student who needed direction came to me and told me that he wanted to graduate cum laude. But with a grade point average of 2.67, he would be lucky to graduate "thank you laude." The student realized that in his younger days, he had not applied himself as he should have. He was determined, however, to be successful. I was able to see that in the way the student carried himself. The support that his mother provided encouraged me to take a chance. I approached some of the teachers he had had in his younger years and asked them to allow him to do extra credit work. The goal: to get his grades changed. One of the assistant principals challenged our efforts, and the fight was on. My instincts clearly told me that this kid was going to make it.

 ALPHONSO THOMPSON
LOGAN HIGH SCHOOL

Whatever assignment they gave me, I made sure that I did two to three times more work so there would be no question about changing the grade. For example, one teacher asked me for a five-page paper on Winston Churchill, and I turned in a seventeen-page paper. Another teacher asked for a three-page paper, and I turned in a ten-page paper. I changed. I changed the way I dressed, acted, and carried myself. I had been known around the campus as the Ultimate Class Clown; I did the most outrageous things on the entire campus of 4,300 people. And nobody took me seriously. I got tired of that label and started buying into Lindsey's direction. Then people started looking at me in a different light. They finally saw me as a smart forensics person who got good grades, and I loved it. My focus had to change because I had to keep up with my current schoolwork, do an enormous amount of extra work on the side, compete at the varsity level on the forensics team, and start at the receiver position on the football team.

Alphonso graduated cum laude. After graduation he was accepted into a state college and graduated from there with honors. Now he is substituting for me at the high school level and is ready to go on to receive his teaching credentials in a year.

It didn't take a miracle to accomplish these things with Terry and Alphonso. There was nothing magical or miraculous. All it took was for me to believe that these students could make it. That, with love and determination, has allowed them to take their rightful places in life.

WHEN THEY GET IT

MIRIAM NALAMUNSI

LOGAN HIGH SCHOOL

Harvard Business School graduate, consultant for MBAs

Everyone always used to say that kids like me didn't need the forensics team or coaches like Mr. Lindsey. By the time I met him at age thirteen, I was already a focused straight-A student from a supportive and well-educated two-parent family.

So people used to ask what benefit a kid like me got from the team other than some training in public speaking.

It is through my experiences on the forensics team that I discovered, and honed, my God-given gift to encourage, motivate, coach, and inspire. I finally got it when I read a book entitled *The Purpose-Driven Life*, which challenged me to consider that my life, my blessings, and my achievements are not about, or for, just me. As I read that book, I realized that the forensics team was really about family. It was about giving and receiving love; it was about planting seeds and watching them grow to harvest. Those of us who came to Mr. Lindsey, to the team, overflowing with love, confidence, hope, and discipline, worked with him to fill up our teammates who came with insufficient supplies of those critical components of success. Winning tournaments and creating speech champions was only a by-product of the real work we did, as a team and a family.

When I think back to my experiences on the team, sure, I was a competitor. But I was also a tutor, an assistant coach, a mentor, a big sister. One semester I was Mr. Lindsey's teacher's assistant, and I worked with one of our teammates in math—a young man the school had written off and handed over to Mr. Lindsey's care as a last resort. I attended math class with him to ensure he understood the material and was behaving. He went on to become a forensics national champion, went to college, and is now a teacher and a father. There is a whole group of young men from our team who, to this day, eight years later, consider me a sister.

And so it was. Those who had, offered, and those who needed, received: love, confidence, coaching, attention. I don't remember being explicitly told that our job was to care for one another, but Mr. Lindsey was such a powerful example for how our team, the James Logan Forensics Team, would work.

He fed kids who didn't have money to eat, he bought them clothes for tournaments and paid their entrance fees, he took them into his home, he took them to church. He even taught me how to drive a stick shift!

Everyone said kids like me didn't need the team or coaches like him.

But they were wrong. I'd say every kid needs a team like ours and a coach like him to learn both the abilities and responsibilities of being a champion in life: lessons about finding sources of strength and support as well as lessons about pouring out what you've been given so that your talents and blessings are not wasted just on you but are multiplied in the lives of those around you.

"REALITY" TEACHING

Randy

Grandma, I couldn't tell if you were singing "You Are My Sunshine" or if you were actually being hurled into the molten sun itself.

—*cartoonist Mark Parisi's caption for "American Idol's Simon Cowell: The Early Years"*

At this writing, "reality" television shows still populate the prime-time airwaves. If behavioral scientists are right about the imitative nature of adolescents, there is reason for concern. Some teenagers, after all, sustained serious injuries after imitating the stunts they observed on MTV's show "Jackass." But the harmful effects go beyond simple imitation. These shows—sometimes characterized as "pop culture poison"—influence a child's perception of what is normal and accepted.

What is the antidote for such poison? A well-informed teacher who doesn't resort to scare tactics or needless exaggeration. Teachers who preach that watching any television is bad for you aren't taken seriously by students. And, worse yet, those teachers are wrong. In his book *Freakonomics*, University of Chicago professor Steven D. Levitt says, "Despite the conventional wisdom, watching television apparently does not turn a child's brain to mush." Levitt gives the example of Finland (ranked as having the world's best education system). In Finland children do not begin school until age seven. Most, however, have learned to read before they enter school by watching American TV with Finnish subtitles.

The pragmatic teacher, therefore, models good judgment. It's much less expensive than, say, moving to Finland. Try recommending worthwhile programs—"House," "Numb3rs," "Gilmore Girls"—that entertain but also teach. Remind students that "reality" television is largely about lies. That's how you become the "survivor." Reality teaching, on the other hand, is about telling students the truth.

Students need to see you as a real person and not just someone playing the role of teacher. Personal revelations bring people closer together. Trust is built. Empathy. When you were an adolescent, you shared some of the same dreams as your students. Share them with your students. Such honesty is endearing. (Unless, of course, you were a child of the 1960s and your dream was to "stick it to the man.") I always tell my students of how I first knew I wanted to become a writer. I say:

> Mine is not the poet's tongue. Not yet. Perhaps when I come back from the university I shall be able to express myself more adequately. Someday—ah, but it is but a dream—someday perhaps I shall be a writer.

Wait. That's not my dream. That's the dream of the lovable character Asa Hearthrug in Max Shulman's book *Barefoot Boy with Cheek*. And when I opened that cheeky book in eighth grade, my life changed forever.

Max spoke directly to me. "Randy," he said (for that was my name), "you can be a successful writer." "Huzzah!" I shouted. "Ahem," Max interrupted, "not as successful as I am but good enough for government work." Max's thoughts tend to blend with my grandfather's sometimes. But I digress (that's for you, Max).

Unfortunately, my high school did not offer many opportunities for growth. My classmates and I, for example, were never assigned papers of literary analysis. A simple plot synopsis would always suffice. My one book review was based on information gleaned from the dust cover. I can't remember the title of the book, but some important-sounding people seemed to like it.

The purpose of sharing this particular tale is twofold: (1) to give the students permission to play with language and (2) to encourage the students to see me as human. The key, of course, is to use these reality teaching stories judiciously. Before I would assign the first paper in any class, I would tell the following story.

On the opening day of my freshman year at the University of Nebraska (a wholly imaginary place, as you know), my English professor gave the following assignment: write a three- to five-page paper on this line from "The Love Song of J. Alfred Prufrock" by T. S. Eliot: "I should have been a pair of ragged claws scuttling across the floors of silent seas." Not having written any papers of literary analysis in high school, I laughed appreciatively. Then I realized all was not play at the University of Nebraska. Back at the dorm, I borrowed a typewriter and three pieces of paper. Treading water in the stream of consciousness, I stroked the keys. Gee, if you were on the floor of the sea, you might drown. Stroke. Stroke.

And, golly, ragged claws must be uncomfortable. Or some such nonsense. When I finally reached the top of the third page, I uncommenced typing.

A week after turning in my masterpiece, the professor returned our papers. That is, he passed out everyone's paper but mine. "That's a fine how-do-you-do," I thought. "The professor lost my first college paper." But I was not so fortunate. At that moment, he produced a stack of papers (actually just my paper photocopied for everyone else in the class). No shouts of "Huzzah!" this time.

As he distributed my work, he said, "In my entire teaching career, this is the single worst paper I have ever read." The fact that he was an older gentleman was not especially reassuring.

But I digress.

I tell my students that I could have reacted in many different ways to the professor's pronouncement. I could have challenged his rudeness. I could have charged out of the classroom in a huff. Or I could have put my head on my desk and wept silently. What I did do, I explain, was listen to his criticism. The professor pointed out that if you have twelve paragraphs on a single page, chances are that you didn't develop any of your ideas. "Hmm," I thought. In fact, every criticism he leveled at my paper had the ring of truth. Still, I wasn't going to let his deskside manner discourage me. No one stole Asa Hearthrug's dream. And no one was going to steal mine.

The purpose of telling the students this story should be self-evident. Any criticism I might level at their papers was now tempered by the students' awareness of my professor's approach. By comparison, the harsh would appear humane. My mere survival gave them hope.

The second story I would tell in every class had another self-evident meaning. In a society where little seems shameful, we need to remind students that some acts go beyond the pale. At the same time, I want the students to understand that we all make mistakes. We all have regrets. What we learn from those experiences is what matters. Yasmin Mashhoon, one of my former students, retold this second story in her essay "The Media as a Freak Show."

YASMIN MASHHOON
ALBUQUERQUE ACADEMY

I was sitting in English class the other day, and my teacher told us a story about his days as a student at the University of Nebraska. Somewhat bored one day, he said, he was lurking in the lunch line at Selleck Quadrangle. So, in order to entertain his friends and the girls behind them, he was doing his best—or, should I say, worst—impression of a mentally challenged person. He was successfully distorting his voice, face, and body when he looked up for a moment, and his eyes locked onto those of a member of the kitchen staff. My teacher described how he felt her eyes pierce right through him as she said, "How would you feel if you really were that way?"

My teacher was immediately ashamed, and he didn't say a word. Standing in that line all those years ago, he was ashamed that he was imitating someone different than he. At that moment, he made a personal decision to stop supporting the Freak Show.

You have to believe that students can learn from the truth. That they can handle the truth. And that is reality teaching.

But I digress.

WHEN THEY GET IT

DAVID LINDSAY-ABAIRE

MILTON ACADEMY

Playwright (works include Fuddy Meers, Kimberly Akimbo, *and the book for* Shrek: The Musical*)*

Randy's laugh. It always took me by surprise. And not just because it was always so sudden and loud, like a small bomb going off in the corner of the classroom, but because it was so honest and immediate. You always knew when Randy was amused. And if you amused Randy, you did good.

I heard that laugh often while rehearsing my humorous interp piece (Larry Shue's *The Nerd*) sometimes by simply hitting the phrase "hideous pagan ritual" in a new way.

In our Current Events/Public Speaking class, while giving a speech about Reagan's economic policies, I remember tossing in an utterly incongruous reference to Zasu Pitts that resulted in peals of laughter from Randy—and no one else in the class.

And in sophomore English, I remember trying to make what I thought was a profound comparison between Holden Caulfield and Vincent van Gogh by way of folksinger Don McLean, when that same explosive giggle stopped me midsentence. I'm still not sure whether Randy was laughing at how clever I was or how insanely foolish I sounded. Either way, it was gratifying.

It was that same year that a classmate got the idea that we should mount a sophomore class play. I remember her turning to me and saying, "And you should write it. Because you're the funny one." And just like that I became a playwright. I was fourteen and knew absolutely nothing about writing plays, but I did it anyway, because someone told me to. Usually that kind of reasoning gets a kid in trouble. Me, I got a career out of it.

That play was called "Mario's House of Italian Cuisine," and it was an insane farce with parts for thirty of my classmates. There were about fifteen different plots, little structure to speak of, and a motley cast of characters that featured hillbillies, lockjawed millionaires, a hot-tempered Spaniard, and a couple mafioso goombahs, all wandering in and out of a seedy restaurant doing God knows what. It was, admittedly, a terrible, terrible play. But that didn't seem to matter.

The audience laughed and cheered and stomped their feet, loving it in a way that most high school audiences love to see a bunch of kids in goofy costumes acting like idiots and having a fun time. The jokes were cheap, ridiculously silly, and painfully sophomoric, which was, I think, excusable, seeing as we *were* sophomores. And the response was gushingly positive. Except, as I remember, from Randy.

When he came to the show, I sat in the audience waiting for that laugh, that distinctive giggle that rose up and cut through all others. I craved to hear it. I wanted Randy's approval desperately. But it never came. Well, actually, it did—the laugh, that is—a couple times, but during the oddest, most random moments in the show, when no one else was laughing. Except maybe me.

After the show I asked Randy what he thought, and he spoke exclusively about that strange character with the multiple-personality disorder who took himself out to dinner and argued with himself about a violent crime he may or may not have committed. "That guy's dialog was so off-kilter, and out of left field, and surprising, and a little dark and disturbing, and absurdly funny, but somehow grounded and honest. Those bits were so . . . you, so David." And then I paused and asked about the other twenty-nine characters, and Randy said something like, "They were fine. They were essentially stereotypes doing stereotypical shtick. And there's nothing wrong with that. Some of the best comedies written have stereotypes at the center of the humor, and people laugh—but they laugh because it's so familiar, and easy, and unsurprising. I like to be surprised. And you're so good at surprising us."

It was, I think, my first review. And boy, was it mixed. And yet, it's still one of the most insightful, constructive, and helpful reviews I've ever received. Of course, we all want raves, but hyperbole doesn't often make us better artists. Randy was able to be supportive and complimentary while being honest and constructive as well. Yes, it was fun to amuse a room full of my friends with a bunch of cheap jokes. But was that all I wanted to do? Couldn't I be funny *and* smart *and* surprising *and* true to my own voice and sensibility? Randy obviously thought so. And he challenged me and made me think about what it was I wanted to accomplish. He aimed me in the right direction.

PRACTICAL MATTERS

A SIT-IN WITH CLASS

The poet W. H. Auden defined a college professor as someone "who talks in other people's sleep." This harsh description may be true for those readers who remember their halcyon college days as a four-year recovery program that didn't quite work. The truth is, though, that the right professor can change the life of a child.

Enter the parent as matchmaker. As your child shows a serious interest in a subject, search a nearby college's catalog for a compatible choice. Courses exist for the next Stephen King, Queen Latifah, or Science Guy. But you don't have to really enroll again (or recover). Just look for a class that is offered in the evenings or on Saturdays. Then find a willing professor—a professor who will allow you and your child to sit in the back of the classroom, like shadows on the wall. Surprisingly, these people exist. Audit the course. The "kindly old Professor Gompers" will be elated to finally have someone in his class who wants to be there.

After class you can take your child to a campus coffeehouse. Talking with your child about what was discussed in class that evening, you can suggest a project that parallels the class assignments, one that the two of you might work on together. In a film studies course, for example, you could write sample dialogue for a screenplay based on your lives—a project guaranteed to bring reality teaching closer to home. And as you toss back your $4 caramel mocha latte, you can look forward to the days when you'll actually be footing tuition bills.

Patching Human Souls

Tommie

Every man must decide whether he will walk in
the light of creative altruism or in the darkness of
destructive selfishness.

—*Martin Luther King Jr.*

Thirty years ago, when I was still young, the three most important institutions for promoting good—the home, the school,
and the churches—all had a major responsibility. The home was
to set the parameters. The church was to establish ethics. The
schools were to teach. As we move into the twenty-first century,
it has been incumbent upon the schools to shoulder much of the
responsibility for the home, in part because 50 percent of the
homes have only a single parent. Many students opt not to attend
church for a number of reasons. The responsibility of setting

parameters, then, is now on us as teachers. In other words, we've become the patchers of human souls.

When I talk about patching human souls, I'm talking about the things we do day to day that help sustain a child. Many students come to us with shattered spirits and deflated confidence. There are so many things that kids have to deal with that I'm amazed they're able to focus on education at all. Many of them find themselves without direction.

 ROBERT HAWKINS
LOGAN HIGH SCHOOL

Situated in the later teenage years, I found myself, as most students do, beset with hubris. I mean, I was in high school now, I was sixteen, and I knew everything! Unfortunately, it was this naivete that did everything but ameliorate my wounds. My soul was hurting.

Sparing the intricacies of the docudrama that was my adolescent life, I remember feeling like no one could understand. Of course, like any good play, the plot twisted. It happened when I casually joined something called forensics. Mr. Lindsey dropped dramatic interp script after dramatic interp script into my lap. These works, coupled with his relentless "badgering" standards, still give me chills.

I think Mr. Lindsey understands the therapy of performing drama. Embodying these characters offered not just escape but companionship. Standing in Room 408, becoming one with a character, allowed my voice to become the organ of my soul. I was able, through empathy, to come into my own. Playwrights August Wilson, Carlyle Brown, Ntozake Shange, and their contemporaries all taught me who I was. And I find myself to this day opening these dramas and reading my own story.

EINSTEIN SIMPLIFIED

I can remember a student—let's call her Rachel—who would come to school every day and was happy to be a part of the forensics team. People were around her and the support system was there. She would always make it a point to try to get my attention. One day Rachel said to me that when she came to school, she was very happy, but when she was at home, she was sad. I asked her why. She told me that her parents had recently been kicked out of their house, and she was living in a one-bedroom apartment with an uncle who was dying of AIDS. It was her responsibility to take care of him until he died, which he did a day before her eighteenth birthday. It was very difficult for her to watch her uncle deteriorate from a healthy man to skin and bones. In fact, for some reason she could not explain, Rachel's uncle didn't even have the tears to cry anymore. There was no happiness for her at home. Consequently, all of her efforts were put into her schooling and her participation on the forensics team. For three years, she earned her way to the state championship. These trips were her escape. The patch that she needed for her spirit was validation—something to sustain her until she could move to the next stage of her life.

Believe it or not, teachers need their souls and spirits patched as well. Sometimes, we can find it right in our classrooms. For example, take Jeff, a student who, at the age of thirteen, discovered he had cancer and eventually had to have a prosthetic femur implant. He did not allow that to stop him from pursuing his education and competing on the forensics team. In fact, he wanted to take on one of the toughest events in forensics, Lincoln-Douglas debate. For two years, he was courageous. But after the chemo treatments got the best of him, he began to decline. I would visit Jeff at his home and at the hospital. Through his hope and his positive outlook on life, my soul was patched. I felt that if he were able to go through those rigorous treatments and still want to write that next term paper, complete his math assignments, and be a part of the forensics program, it would be nothing for me to get up every morning to come to school and teach others.

Jeff's goal was to graduate from high school and attend his senior ball—both were achieved. I remember my last time visiting Jeff. The nurses in the hospital ward said that he was so proud to be a part of the James Logan Forensics Team. Even though I had to deal with the bureaucracy of the administration and the tedious tasks necessary to be a forensics coach, I was able to gain strength while he was losing his. I hope it made me a better person. I hope it made me appreciate life. And I hope his life has inspired me to never give up. Jeff was the validation for what I do every day, and he truly was a patch for my human soul.

WHEN THEY GET IT

ALPHONSO THOMPSON

LOGAN HIGH SCHOOL

Substitute teacher

One moment that sticks in my head to this day is the day we lost the state championship held at Long Beach State. It came down to a tiebreaker for my partner and me and another team. We were reigning state champions in duo interpretive as freshmen, and the other team was seniors. They gave the tiebreaker to the other team, because my partner and I had won the year before and we still had two years of competition left. I was completely crushed by this decision, but I said nothing and simply smiled. My partner and I had worked so hard and I had dedicated that year to the memory of my grandmother, who passed one month before the tournament. Mr. Lindsey and I both cried in the restroom in the lobby of our hotel when he told me what happened. He said, "Remember this moment—you are a man now. You keep your head up and don't let anyone see you cry. You take victory the same as defeat. That's class, and that is what separates champions from everyone else."

When I got home, my mother told me that my aunt Trina had lost her battle with breast cancer, and I felt like the loneliest person in the world. But at my aunt's funeral, Mr. Lindsey and a bunch of my teammates were there to give me support. We became a close family and still are to this day. I didn't have a father in my household. Mr. Lindsey was the closest thing to being my father.

He is more than a teacher. He is a father figure to every student he comes in contact with. He never needed any money from anyone, because his reward from helping people and saving lives (like mine) is much greater than material things.

WALL-FLOWERING

Randy

Me not cool. Me totally room temperature.

—*Joan, "Joan of Arcadia"*

On one episode of the television show "Joan of Arcadia," Joan pulls another high school student from the path of an oncoming truck. Suddenly, she is showered with the unwanted attention of the girl she saved. The attention of her classmates. Her teachers. The high school principal even suggests to Joan that her act of heroism is "an oasis in the desert of your permanent record." Joan, bothered by this attention, prefers her former life as a wallflower. For those of you not familiar with the show, God, in various disguises, speaks to Joan. God explains to Joan that the saved girl needs a hero, that some people can't see their own lights. They live in a kind of darkness. They think that the only way they can see is by using the lights of others.

29

The lesson for Joan is about the paradoxical nature of life. For far too many students, the most difficult choice is between what they know they ought to do and what they see other students doing. They are comfortable in the darkness, but they seek the light. A teacher's job is to help students find peace within these contradictions.

The shell must break before the bird can fly.

—*Alfred, Lord Tennyson*

If you weren't a wallflower at junior high dances, chances are that you know people who were. This form of shyness can follow someone into adulthood, and the resulting social barriers can seem insurmountable. Don't confuse the fear of public speaking, however, with shyness. A reluctance to speak up in class is not necessarily a symptom of shyness. Almost all students fear public speaking. Only some of those students are shy. The painfully shy need immediate attention. Painfully shy students usually are excessively self-conscious. For me, five strategies have proved useful in reducing their suffering.

1. *Create a supportive classroom environment.* I always require all students to applaud enthusiastically after any oral presentation. I joke that the applause is to confuse the performing student into thinking that he or she has succeeded. The real purpose, however, is to confuse the performing student into thinking he or she has succeeded. Clever, eh? Success experiences are one temporary antidote for shyness.

2. *Teach in small steps when possible.* In a speech class, my first assignment is to give a one-minute introduction for any

topic. I provide sample topics to ease the natural concern over what is appropriate.

3. *Provide blueprints to help students know what is expected.* If students are to write a persuasive essay, provide exemplary ones for them to read. My experience is that students learn best from examples. Annotated examples give students that blueprint to follow.

4. *Have former speech class students provide demonstrations to increase belief in oneself.* Care must be taken, though, not to intimidate the less experienced or shy students. Videotaping willing students builds a library of choices for later viewing. The shy students need to see that success is possible.

5. *Give students time to think.* Less pressure, less pain. When the student does respond, positive reinforcement and useful feedback make all the difference.

WHEN THEY GET IT

CANDACE KOONTZ

LOGAN HIGH SCHOOL

Cal State Hayward student

It was during a trip to Nevada-Union High School that I was able to see clearly for the first time what forensics really meant to me. I remember I performed my piece for about 250 of the kids, and at that time, I thought it was a good performance, but later I came to learn it was not just a good performance, it was a motivator.

After Mr. Lindsey finished talking to the kids, we were on our way out when I noticed a young girl crying as she watched us leave. I approached her, and in her hand was a perfect sketch of me while I performed. The sketch in its use of detail showed so much life between those simple lines. She clearly was talented beyond her own knowledge; at least, that's what I would imagine Mr. Lindsey saying. That young girl then asked me to autograph the sketch, and she told me that as she watched me perform, she realized that she, too, was special just like me. It was hard for me to hold back the tears; here was this beautiful young girl who had no self-confidence, when she should be radiating pride in herself.

Before forensics I was that same girl, afraid of myself, afraid of the world judging me, and, most important, afraid to try for fear of failing. But now, the confidence Mr. Lindsey had in me from the beginning is my own.

IMPROBABLE DREAMS

Tommie

Some people see things as they are and say,
"Why?" I dream things that never were and say,
"Why not?"

—Robert F. Kennedy's paraphrase of
George Bernard Shaw

The Broadway musical *Spamalot* reminds us that Eric Idle's hands are the devil's playthings. *Camelot*, the inspiration for Idle's playfulness, reminds us that once there was a time. . . . As for me, I can't hear the word *Camelot* without thinking about the Kennedys: the mythic connection that idealized the hopes of a different era. Before he was assassinated in 1968, Robert F. Kennedy would end every campaign trail speech by echoing Shaw's "Why not?"

That belief in what is possible captures the spirit of my student Jerri Kay-Phillips. She lived the improbable dream. As a competitor in our program, Jerri had the ability to win, no matter what the circumstances. Always a team player, Jerri made some particularly memorable contributions one year at the Cal Invitational. As she competed in a Lincoln-Douglas debate round, the team discovered that in order for us to win the overall sweepstakes award, Jerri would likely have to beat three young men—all from the same prestigious private school—in consecutive rounds. When Steve Wilson, who was our coach for L-D debate at the time, approached her and explained the situation, Jerri looked at him and said, "Well, I guess I'll have to go kick some butt."

Jerri recalls that many of the competitors she had competed with in early rounds had gotten together to come up with strategies to dismantle her arguments. The odds and her opponents were against her. Walking into the room for her quarterfinal round, Jerri immediately felt the effects of a packed room: the air circulation was poor, and the stifling heat made it difficult to think, let alone come up with persuasive arguments. But Jerri was determined. She knew that her commitment could make a difference for the team—she had to come through. After winning the quarterfinal round, she walked outside to get some air, waiting nervously for her next opponent. I knew she was hoping for an easier round. Being familiar with the private school, however, she was well aware that her next two rounds would be even more difficult. Studying the posted results, Jerri found out who her semifinal opponent would be. She remembered beating him before, but that was at a smaller tournament—the stakes at this tournament were much higher. But her cross-examination expertise helped her defeat the highly skilled debater.

The final round was next, and now she knew that nothing was going to stand between her and the Berkeley championship. Even more determined, she was victorious, and our team won the sweepstakes award by a mere five points. I truly believe that Jerri's example gave our team the impetus to move toward winning a state championship.

JERRI KAY-PHILLIPS
LOGAN HIGH SCHOOL

The Rotary Club in California hosts its own speech competition for cash prizes, so Mr. Lindsey chose three of us to speak before the club to see what we could do. Fortunately, I won the first competition, earning $100, which I put away toward my college fund. The next competition was a little more challenging, but I came away with the $250 prize. After winning the third competition and a whopping $500, I was given the great news that I would be competing for the $1,000 Rotary Club grand prize in Monterey, California. I was ecstatic at the opportunity, but there was one problem—it happened on the same day as the forensics state championships.

I was torn about what to do. Should I take the all-expense-paid trip to Monterey with premier accommodations and a chance at $1,000, or should I compete with my team at state champs? Mr. Lindsey obviously wanted me to compete with the team, and I wanted to be there, too. But with one sister already in college and a brother one year younger than me, college was going to be a financial burden on my family, and I wanted to help in any way that I could. Mr. Lindsey said, "Jerri, if you go to state champs, you can win the whole thing." I said, "I know, Mr. Lindsey, but I've been to state for the past three years, and now I've got to think about my future."

My parents were also divided, with my dad urging me to support the team and my mom telling me to prepare financially for college. Addressing this dilemma, Mr. Lindsey took action. He said, "Jerri, we will raise that money for you. I don't want you to have to worry about money, so you compete with the team and we'll make up the difference." With that, Mr. Lindsey began his own fund-raising campaign among the teachers and staff at Logan to raise the money that I would have earned from the Rotary Club. And while the final total still fell short, it was worth it because I had the opportunity to compete with my team.

As we began the rounds at Stockton Junior College, I was sure that I had made the right decision. I wondered what it would have been like to stay in the fabulous hotel and speak before the Rotary Club members, but as I faced each competitor in debate and gave each speech for extemp, I knew that I would much rather be speaking before my peers than a group I hardly knew. I ground my way through the competition and found myself in the final round of Lincoln-Douglas debate before a packed audience. We were debating about civil disobedience, and when my opponent argued that we should be more like Dr. Martin Luther King and not break the law, I pounced. I told the crowded room, "Perhaps my opponent never read Dr. King's famous 'Letter from Birmingham Jail,' where he was in *jail* for breaking the law as he practiced civil disobedience!" I won the round on a 7–0 decision.

I had not seen this kind of drive in a team in a long time—they were destined. At the state tournament, Jerri led the way with her dual championship in extemporaneous speaking and Lincoln-Douglas debate. As a graduate of Stanford University, Jerri has taken her improbable dream into the world, where her heart and desire make a difference every day. And I think about that difference every day. All of the students who walk into my classroom have improbable dreams. For them, the odds must seem overwhelmingly against them. My job is to change the odds.

And now for something completely different.

WHEN THEY GET IT

JAMES TITUS HARRIS

LOGAN HIGH SCHOOL

Florida Agricultural and Mechanical University student

Throughout my time in forensics (1997–2001), I learned many things about life: how to deal with adversity, criticism, hate, racism, and different personalities, just to name a few. However, these lessons do not come close to the lesson I finally learned in college at Florida A&M University. As I look back at my time in high school, there is one comment that I remember Mr. Lindsey saying almost on a daily basis, if not to me, then to some other person on the team: "You don't get it now, but one day you'll look back and get it." I would listen to this and, honestly, shrug it off. I did not understand what "it" was and how I couldn't understand "it" while I was in high school.

I spent years trying to understand what he meant about getting "it." Then one day during my sophomore year in college, as I sat in the front of the room of an engineering course, my professor began making comments about my attitude toward the class by saying that even though I was making good grades, I was not taking the class seriously. I responded with a typically arrogant type of attitude, and the next thing out of his mouth was what allowed me to finally grasp the most important lesson Mr. Lindsey ever taught me. My professor told me that I was not going to make it, that I was not going to amount to anything.

At that moment, I realized what "it" was. I realized that throughout my life there had never been anyone, other than my parents, to believe in me and fight for my dreams. I realized that in life the majority of people are not out to help you succeed but to watch you fail. In high school, there was never a time that Mr. Lindsey lost faith in me or gave up on me. I was spoiled. I thought I was supposed to be taken care of by others. It was not until I was out on my own, facing adversity, that I could fully appreciate what Mr. Lindsey had taught me: that my dream was *my* responsibility.

To me, "it" is Mr. Lindsey, a true blessing in my life. It is not every day that a young African-American man can meet another African-American man willing to put his neck on the line for him, willing to fight for him, and willing to speak up for him.

CONSIDERING THE SOURCE

Randy

A weekday edition of the *New York Times* contains more information than the average person was likely to come across in a lifetime in seventeenth-century England.

—*Richard Saul Wurman*

There is a grave danger presenting itself to today's classroom teacher: who is providing the information, the content? *Boston Globe* columnist Ellen Goodman argues that "everybody is talking about 'content' as if there were a spigot somewhere to fill up the electronic jar."

Goodman has a point. Students often assume that because the information comes from the Internet, then it must be correct and current. Unfortunately, these students don't realize that good content gathering takes time. The lazy gatherer makes mis-

"GRANTED, WE HAVE TO DO THE RESEARCH. AND WE CAN DO SOME RESEARCH ON THE RESEARCH. BUT I DON'T THINK WE SHOULD GET INVOLVED IN RESEARCH ON RESEARCH ON RESEARCH."

takes at the speed of cyberspace. Anyone, after all, can publish on the Internet. The reliability and quality of information is often in question. A gym teacher, for example, can dribble on and on in cyberspace—and the student may have no defense, no way to hand check his or her credentials.

Clearly, students must learn to evaluate Internet research for accuracy, authority, objectivity, currency, and coverage. As technology speeds up the distribution of thoughts, students must be more responsible for the painstaking process of thinking about what they mean. In a sense, students must become investigative journalists who sift through the facts to report only what is true. Goodman is right: "A journalist is to a content provider as a farmer is to a waiter. They're both in the food biz. But the farmer is the one to count on."

But "considering the source" has far-reaching implications. In the same way that students give too much credence to information found on the Internet, they often have too much faith in the feedback they receive from teachers. What the students learn about research should be applied to their own lives. Not all criticism of them or their work will be fair. Students must understand context and bias. And sometimes, whether they think it's fair or not, people are simply unpleasant. When I hand papers back to students, I always ask them to consider what I said but to remember that I could be wrong. I share with them some of the numerous stories of writers who were turned down by publishers. Or I read a scathing review or two of the work of one of their favorite writers.

The irreverent Dorothy Parker is a student favorite. In Parker's *New Yorker* column "Constant Reader," she offered a four-word review of A. A. Milne's classic *Winnie the Pooh*: "Tonstant weader fwowed up."

Knowing that someone skewered poor Winnie usually makes students feel better. And more prepared for the criticism they will inevitably receive. Debunking destructive criticism is a survival skill that all students need.

At the same time, students have to be careful of people who only tell them what they want to hear. Some friends are not friends at all. These sources of information will say anything to gain approval. Students must learn that honesty often comes with a price to pay.

 BEN UNANAOWO
LOGAN HIGH SCHOOL

My whole life I was desperately longing to be adored and admired, keeping hangers-on in my presence for the enjoyment of having my ego stroked. Initially, I got that same buzz from winning tournaments, but I think I finally changed during my senior year of high school. Aware of my deception and lies, Mr. Lindsey had the choice to shun me or to embrace my immaturity. With a whole new attitude adjustment, we were able to make one last run at success. But the first real success I had was in performing for church folk and people in the community. And as my teammate Pierre and I finished one performance of the play *The Meeting*—about the lives of Martin Luther King Jr. and Malcolm X—an older woman approached us with tears in her eyes, telling us her late husband had marched with Dr. King and she felt very moved by what she had seen.

I became aware of the power and importance of the communicator not just in the community but also in society. Martin Luther King, Malcolm X, César Chávez—all were able to change problems in society with their intellect and communication. Although Mr. Lindsey's contributions to society aren't on that grand of a stage, this past summer he helped a young dark-skinned kid speak in front of four thousand people in a building where African-Americans were once not allowed to enter.

Keep away from people who try to belittle your ambitions. Small people always do that, but the really great make you feel that you, too, can become great.

—*Mark Twain*

WHEN THEY GET IT

CHRIS MARIANETTI

ALBUQUERQUE ACADEMY

Musician, composer

Charles Mingus always believed that turning something simple into something complex was easy but that finding a way of making something complicated into something simple, something "awesomely" simple, was true creativity. Randy, in my mind, has *always* understood that.

My own "moment" in high school came when I decided to take a speech about thinking in an uncommon way and combine it with the cartoon strip *Calvin and Hobbes*. I remember, in fact, the very time I first presented this idea to Randy. We were walking down to the school library, on our way to his English/speech class, and I told him that my oratory needed more structure and clarity and so I was thinking of using the different frames of a *Calvin and Hobbes* cartoon I had found to guide and flag-mark my various arguments and points. Each paragraph would correspond to the caption of the relevant frame of the cartoon. I really didn't know what he would think of this, and, to be honest, nor did I expect much of a reaction because our speechwriting class was quite large and there were plenty of other kids, far brighter than myself, who could speak both improvisationally and at length about, let's say, the current political climate in Zaire while at the same time throwing in words like *incongruous* and *titillating*. Well, he listened to this muddled seed of an idea and when I finished stopped me and told me in an ever-so-sincere way that *this* was brilliant.

And then he got really excited and went off on one of his creative splurges, showering me with ideas for developing this theme and using the cartoon and on and on, though now I really don't remember much of that. But I remember him telling me that *this* was so brilliant. And I have to admit that I was both shocked and touched. As a sophomore, I hadn't really thought that I could be brilliant or that anything I could think of could be brilliant. So as far as I could figure, there were several possible scenarios here: (1) Randy was exaggerating so as to make me feel like less of the nerd that I truly was; (2) he had *actually* said that this was so "Berlaimont," referring, of course, to the small northern French town's odd obsession with *Calvin and Hobbes* cartoons; or (3) he actually thought my idea was brilliant. I hoped it was the latter.

It turns out that he *did* think my idea was brilliant, and, because of this, *I* began to think my idea was brilliant. And so I wrote a somewhat decent speech based on a clever little structural idea. In retrospect, the speech was not unbelievable and certainly not, for that matter, unbeatable, but it had this idea—this idea about structure. The idea was a way to take a garbled mess of quotes, opinions, and arguments and structure them into something perceptible, so that "they" (the audience) would get it. The idea was about making something complicated seem simple. For this reason, it was creative; for this reason, it was, in Randy's words, "brilliant." He saw this and he encouraged it.

Now I write music. And my compositions all seem to carry and develop the seed of this idea. In the "academia" of contemporary composition, it's quite easy to be complicated and to write complex music. For composers now, all the old rules of composition and structure have, in the last century of music, been broken or at least bent beyond most recognition. The challenge then, as I see it, is how to write a new piece of music that is graspable, that is perceptible. How to make a garbled mess of notes, chords, and harmonies into something understandable and perceivable on more than just one level, because we all listen to music differently and we all understand it and feel it in different ways. And to do this, to succeed in doing this, is what I struggle for.

To me as a high school speech student, this day walking down to the library telling Randy about my idea didn't seem all that important. Looking back now, however, I can see that this was a piece of that seed. And Randy helped instill in me, through writing orations, a way of thinking that has shaped how I write and think of music today. For that I am truly grateful.

SELF-REFILLING PROPHECIES

Randy

> Like I always say, there's no *I* in team. But there is a *me* if you jumble it up.
>
> —*Dr. Gregory House, "House"*

As a medical Sherlock Holmes, the misanthropic but brilliant diagnostician Dr. Gregory House is not exactly a people person. Hugh Laurie, the actor who portrays House, explains his self-absorbed characterization this way: "In this touchy-feely age, reason is not a popular thing. Facts are not popular things. Logic is not a popular thing. Warmth and emotion and sympathy are popular things." Maybe Laurie is onto something.

At a seminar I attended on the topic of self-fulfilling prophecy, the presenter began by writing the following on the chalkboard: "I am not what I think I am. I am not what you think I am. I am what I think you think I am." This mirror effect influences, for good or ill, every student. In other words, when teachers expect students to do well and demonstrate intellectual growth, they do; when teachers do not have these expectations, performance and growth suffer.

Researchers often refer to Harvard professor Robert Rosenthal's famous Oak School experiment, also known as the Pygmalion effect. Rosenthal found significant spurts in intellectual growth in elementary-age students when more was expected of them. Students who were expected to succeed at a higher level demonstrated marked improvement. Students in the control group fell behind. Although the results of the study seem fairly self-evident, they received much criticism—perhaps because educational psychologists had no solutions for the problem of self-fulfilling prophecies. Professor Rosenthal admits he didn't know what to do with the findings.

Clearly, teachers need to be aware of the consequences of their expectations. Picture a kindergarten student's initial fling with fingerpaints, her masterpiece a swirling blur of flesh strokes reminiscent of van Gogh's earless period—a "Scary Night" if ever there was one. After a cursory glance at the work, the kindergarten teacher says something meant to be comforting: "Nice try, dear." But the young artist knows what she means. Your van Gogh just up and van Went. And another child quits trying, to borrow a line from Ferlinghetti, "too soon, too soon."

Teachers must be careful, though. You don't want to mislead students. As you encourage them, you don't want to give them false hopes. While students must know that we believe in them and in their dreams, they need to be certain that we can be trusted to tell them the truth. In the short-lived television show "Wonderfalls," the disaffected Gen-Y protagonist is asked, "What happens if you take a butterfly out of the cocoon too soon?" She replies, "You get a worm with flippers."

That flippin' possibility is why I always employ self-*refilling* prophecies rather than self-*fulfilling* prophecies. The *self-refilling prophecy* is a term I coined to describe what students should say to themselves to struggle out of their cocoons successfully.

Consider the McCutcheon corollary: "I am not what I think I am. I am not what you think I am. I become what I tell myself I can." Students need to repeatedly refill their tanks with what is possible, no matter what others think. I first learned this lesson while watching "Leave It to Beaver." In this particular episode, Whitey and Beaver are raking their teacher Miss Landers's yard. Whitey asks the Beav if he isn't worried about some of the guys thinking that they're trying to butter up Miss Landers. Beaver replies, "My father says it doesn't matter what other people think of you, only what you think of yourself."

Now repeat that. Even if you have to jumble it up.

WHEN THEY GET IT

MATT BARRETT

ALBUQUERQUE ACADEMY

Stanford University graduate, high school teacher

It was a little surprising to hear Randy say he abhorred jokes that other people had written, partly because I couldn't conceive of any other kind of joke. He preferred a line he created himself to one that someone else had already spun. To a high school student for whom Ferris Bueller was the fountainhead of wit, Randy's attitude was vexing. To someone who later wanted to learn to write, it was finally illuminating.

I had put forth feeble attempts at essays since sometime before sixth grade, but my real introduction to writing came as a competitive public speaker in eleventh grade. I never quite grasped that writing was not an independent act but one that required engaging with an audience until that audience was standing right in front of me, consuming my words as I created them. It was then, too, that all my teachers' warnings about the importance of an introduction became apparent, as I saw that if I couldn't woo my judges in fifteen seconds, I would never woo them in seven minutes.

Given the stress and importance of the opening act, my competitors found ways to avoid it. Instead of using something relevant to the topic, they used the same opening every time, one they knew they could deliver flawlessly. A representatively awful but sadly realistic example was an overwrought, vaguely lyrical anecdote about how, on the African plains, the challenge of survival required antelopes to outrun lions and lions to outrun antelopes, such that everyone had to be running. Speakers used such schlock to introduce speeches on AIDS in Johannesburg, on starvation in Sudan, or on the economy in Malawi. Or, on a really bad day, on Canadian health care. It didn't matter—everyone knew we'd be judged on whether we stuttered and not on our erudition or wit.

Randy stressed that relevance and originality were far more important qualities. It was OK that the first time I went on stage I lost miserably to someone who had rehearsed her introduction before drawing her topic and that bored judges penalized intelligence if it was unrehearsed. Ultimately, Randy taught us, we would outshine our competitors if we learned how to master the very difficult task of writing a brand-new speech in less than thirty minutes. And that, more important, we would earn the respect of the learned audience and gain the self-satisfaction of producing something all our own.

The best way to make a group of sixteen-year-olds laugh was to quote a movie or, with the right group of sixteen-year-olds, to quote Mencken. But it was no way to become a successful comedian, since Mencken, as it turned out, had already published. The best way to win a competition your first time out was to rely on used material to deliver a fluid speech. But it was no way to become a writer. I wasn't sure at first why Randy didn't like used jokes because I hadn't truly begun to crave my own thoughts. Then I learned that relying on used material was too easy a tool. My willingness to produce something really bad, and to recite it in public, was critical to my development as a writer. It was the only way I learned to write anything good.

Safety First

Tommie

Out of this nettle, danger, we pluck this flower, safety.

—*William Shakespeare*

always believed that it is the responsibility of teachers to provide an environment that is safe for kids. That safety means not only physical safety but also the safety necessary to promote learning. Students should feel safe from one another and feel that they can express their views without fear of ridicule or being ostracized. If one is able to provide this kind of classroom setting, there is no doubt that students will not only enjoy school but also enjoy learning. When students find the classroom to be a safe environment, they express their beliefs and feelings freely. Marva Collins explains why this is important:

Trust yourself. Think for yourself. Act for yourself. Speak for yourself. Be yourself. Imitation is suicide.

High school can be dangerous for teenagers when there are so many people there seeking acceptance. The search for acceptance is what drives some students to inflict their own feelings of pain, both emotionally and physically, on others and more often on themselves. Nico, one of my students, was given the opportunity to lessen his pain when he joined the James Logan Forensics Team. There, he was able to turn his fear of being different and his previously inhibited nature into proudly expressing his views to the class. When students are allowed to open up and become themselves, they are able to build the self-esteem that some high school students never attain. Nico faced much ridicule as he searched within to find his identity, but he has now allowed himself to open up to his peers and let them understand who he is.

Because Nico was allowed to trust himself, think for himself, act for himself, speak for himself, and be himself, it saved him from what countless numbers of other gay teens go through: suicide by imitation.

WHEN THEY GET IT

NICHOLAS PARRILLA

LOGAN HIGH SCHOOL

Until my junior year, I remember trying desperately to disguise my true personality by imitating what I felt everyone thought was a typical male. I knew that I wasn't really good at it because even before middle school I was accused of being gay, and people would attach so many negative connotations toward it, forcing me to deny it to attempt to save my reputation. When this carried over to high school and people were still mocking the existence of homosexuality, I began to feel like I wasn't entitled to happiness. My peers convinced me to think that I was plagued with some difficult-to-cure disease, and that would eat at my confidence and self-respect, which I noticed happened to other gay people I knew about.

I watched my boyfriend, for example, drop out of school and become addicted to various drugs after our relationship. I believe it happened because being gay didn't seem to promise him anything productive when he was forced to hide his sexuality to please conservative minds. Had I not been sitting in the forensics room, I would not have given myself a second chance at life to correct my attitude. Pressures of school and social acceptance started to get the best of me because I allowed people to dictate to me that I needed to be a person who was uniform to "normal" people.

Through Mr. Lindsey's words of experience, I learned that a person's worth is the value of his ability to do good for others. People must be strong and voice their opinions in the face of others, even those who oppose those beliefs. He taught me so many things that made me think about becoming a person with higher self-esteem. I felt comfortable to come out to people in my senior year because I knew that I did not have anything to fear, because Mr. Lindsey stressed the importance of supporting one another. Coming out to my team was very painless because I felt respected by my teammates, which enabled me to feel much more at ease with myself. I was no longer willing to hide myself. I was able to be proud. I hope others who are like I was then, close to the point of questioning the purpose for living, are able to reexamine their self-worth and save themselves from failing in life.

THE SECOND TRUTH

CLASS IS
NEVER DISMISSED

CLASS IS
NEVER DISMISSED

Randy

> Whatever you do, Randy, try to avoid eating in
> public.
>
> —*Grandma Amy*

These were my grandma's parting words as I left for my freshman year in college. Other grandmothers might have said, "Study hard" or "Have fun." But not mine. She abhorred public displays of affliction. She had, after all, witnessed—in her kitchen—some of my best gravy slurping. Fries flying through the air. And the raucous red stares (which doesn't really make sense, but you get the idea).

More than once she explained to me her method for hiring the waitresses who wanted to work in her restaurant. First, she would ask the applicant to walk across the room. "They must," Grandma would say, "walk with a sense of purpose." Second, she would examine the heels of the applicant's shoes to see if they were polished. "A person," Grandma would say, "must have pride in their appearance."

When I told Tommie about Grandma's philosophy on pride, he shared with me a passage from the book *Black Pearls*, by Eric V. Copage. Copage writes, "The way we present ourselves to the world has an impact. . . . On this day, I'll take an extra few minutes to look in the mirror and determine if the message I'm projecting is one that I am proud of and that I feel to be me. If not, I will take one concrete action—iron my blouse, change my tie—so that I do feel I am projecting who I am and what I feel."

Something my grandma knew that every student should learn. If you want people to take you seriously, then you must take yourself seriously. Taking yourself seriously is a lesson that is at the heart of this truth: Class Is Never Dismissed. I thought again about my grandma's wisdom as I listened to Jamie Foxx's Oscar acceptance speech for his role in the film *Ray*. Foxx said that his grandmother was his first "acting" teacher:

Stand up straight. Put your shoulders back. Act like you've got sense.

My grandma would have liked that.

You Can't Always Want What You Get

Randy

I can't get no satisfaction.

—*Mick Jagger and Keith Richards*

If Mick and Keith were a bit more epigrammatical, the Stones might have had another greatest hit. Lyrics that include wanting what you get, however, might be difficult for most students to sing along to. They want to win at everything and they want it now. But students face many rites of passage. Some work out. Some don't. Success in life shouldn't be about getting satisfaction—it should be about earning it.

Clearly, self-esteem is important to healthy development. Building self-esteem, though, is not about showering students with empty praise. In his book *Dumbing Down Our Kids: Why*

America's Children Feel Good About Themselves but Can't Read, Write, or Add, Charles Sykes argues that with "the help of goofy textbooks, watered-down requirements and 'recentered' test grade scales, American students have come to value feeling good about a subject over being good in it."

Discussing how to develop a sense of self-worth in students has become a kind of national pastime among educators. The research, however, shows that our efforts at improving self-esteem have not increased academic progress. Clearly, we want students to believe in themselves. What we don't want is the indiscriminate promoting of self-esteem in students just for being themselves.

 AUSTAN GOOLSBEE
MILTON ACADEMY

To become a man in the ancient African Lesu tribe, a boy had to dodge burning branches hurled at him by his father. To become a woman in the Tlingit culture, a girl had to live for an entire year in a dark room, sewing and plucking duck feathers. In New Zealand a youth had to take a knife, venture into the ocean, and kill a shark. And for the Ubatu, the challenge was slaughtering a wild boar, using a wooden spike.

Today such rites of passage seem utterly ridiculous. Yet every year, two million of America's youth engage in their own barbaric rite. Herded into crowded assembly rooms, huddled behind tiny desks, armed with only two soft lead pencils, these adolescents embark on a perilous mission: to choose the best of 3,600 possible ovals, as they undergo three hours of rigorous torture. That's right, they take the Scholastic Aptitude Test—the SAT.

Of course, the format of the SAT has changed somewhat since Austan attacked its legitimacy for measuring academic potential. The required essay makes this rite even more subjective today. The test is supposed to measure learning potential. Sadly, it does little to evaluate the student who does well because of hard work. Therefore, teachers and parents must remind students that a low score on the SAT—or the ACT, for that matter—does not mean that the student is roadkill on the highway of life.

Teaching students that working hard pays off is what we should do. We must lead, not mislead. Students must learn that they can't always get what they want, that true satisfaction is found in ways other than winning. The willingness to fail repeatedly is an attribute that will better serve a student throughout his or her life. A sense of humor helps, too. Our speech team motto was "We know no fear. We know nothing."

Can we ever change our society's obsession with being number one? Probably not. But we can try, one student at a time.

Some luck lies in not getting what you thought you wanted but getting what you have, which once you have got it you may be smart enough to see is what you would have wanted had you known.

—*Garrison Keillor*

WHEN THEY GET IT

JASON WESBECHER

ALBUQUERQUE ACADEMY

Software sales executive

Jason is quick to say how he resigned himself to the life of a semifinalist. Not exactly. Jason earned a $12,000 scholarship as a finalist in the American Legion Oratorical Contest, and he placed third in oratory at the Catholic Nationals. Here he recalls the paradoxical nature of competition.

I could tell you about how Randy taught me to present complex ideas in a meaningful way (which, in essence, is my job today). Or about how he taught me the art of persuasion (which gave me my wife). Or about how I learned argumentation (which is useful in the aforementioned wife department).

I could tell you—with conviction—about how learning all of these things in high school pays dividends on a daily basis for me today. But instead, I am going to tell you about how Randy taught me to fail. (Ironic, given that my junior year oratory was on the quintessential lovable loser himself, Charlie Brown.) What's paradoxical about these moments in high school is that when you are actually "in" the moment, it doesn't seem like much of a moment at all. It's really a moment in retrospect.

My failure moments in retrospect involve underachievement in speech competitions. You see, for three years straight, I was in nearly every semifinal round of every oratory competition of national consequence—emphasis on *semi*. I consistently peaked at eighth or ninth place in every tournament. Always a bridesmaid, never a bride!

Now, let's be clear: this is not such a terrible fate. But my coach and I had an unspoken agreement that we would strive for excellence and would not be satisfied until we achieved our objective. On Saturday afternoons, the final-round names would be posted on a piece of construction paper in the cafeteria. Not only would there not be a Wesbecher on the list, but I wouldn't even experience that split-second euphoria of seeing a last name that remotely resembled mine (no *W*s, and nary a *V*). I would instantly look to my mentor for his reaction, mainly to see how to model my own. And every time, without fail, the reaction would be the same: a big goofy smile and a very bad pun.

Instead of overt consolation, I received an understated but charming brush-off. And you know what? That's exactly how the cookie crumbles fifteen years later. When you set a goal of "excellence"—a goal that only you can measure—you'll find that you fail more often than you succeed. But that's what it takes. You have to be willing to fail to succeed. And it's helpful to pull out a big goofy smile from time to time.

IMAGE ISN'T EVERYTHING, BUT IT'S SOMETHING

Tommie

If *A* is a success in life, then *A* equals *X* plus *Y* plus *Z*. Work is *X*; *Y* is play; and *Z* is keeping your mouth shut.

—*Albert Einstein*

As Einstein suggests, there are unique formulas for success. Many television viewers may remember an advertising campaign a few years ago starring tennis great Andre Agassi. In the commercial, Agassi sells a Nikon camera with the tagline "Image is everything." Whereas for Agassi image may be everything when he's in front of the camera, it certainly isn't everything for him. I've grown to admire and respect this outstanding man for the work he has done, not only for his sport but for his community.

I've had an opportunity to visit Agassi Prep in Las Vegas, and I was truly impressed by the program that he funds for inner-city youth. While kids must be academically responsible, more important, they are encouraged to believe in themselves. I'm no tennis star—even though I'm a former hacker—but I've also embraced the Agassi philosophy to help kids believe in themselves.

We begin with the image they project. I've often instructed my students that they cannot wear wave caps or have their pants sagging during tournaments because it is imperative that they carry themselves in a way that is respectful. The old adage is that the first impression is the lasting impression. Since many students on my team cannot afford suits, and those who could would buy gaudy green and pink suits, I opted to establish a dress code. I wanted everyone to dress in black suits, white shirts, and nice ties. It's a classy look. It makes image appear not as everything but as something. A former student, Puja, explains why image was important to her.

 PUJA BHATIA
LOGAN HIGH SCHOOL

As soon as I walked into the room of my first round of my very first tournament, I immediately noticed fellow competitors and judges inspecting me from the moment I opened the door until the second I sat down in a chair. When it was my turn to speak, they stared intently at me for the first few minutes, not necessarily because they were genuinely interested in what I had to say but because they wanted to catch any mistake in the way I presented myself. Anything from a wrinkled suit to out-of-place hair could be a potential reason for judges to drop a ranking or to be written off as a nonthreat by fellow competitors. Besides the natural butterflies fluttering in my stomach from the nervousness of public speaking for the first time, the glares from the audience made me feel like I had fifty pounds resting on my shoulders.

From that experience, I will never forget how much Mr. Lindsey emphasized that we be equipped not only with professional behavior but also with perfectly ironed black suits. I didn't understand why the way we dressed mattered so much until we walked into a tournament in a formation that people called "the black cloud." We walked into a tournament, and people knew Logan High School had arrived. We clapped for every person who took first place and people imitated. We walked into our rooms with confidence, and judges took notice. It was because Mr. Lindsey told us the way we present ourselves is just as important as the content of our speech that we changed from high school students to young adults. And that was why people gave us the respect that he worked so hard to help us obtain.

In a world that is so fiercely competitive, I teach my students that the first impression is so poignantly important because, oftentimes, they don't get a second chance. Many of my students have told me that forensics had by far given them the most valuable education they needed in all aspects of how they presented themselves. After Puja's first tournament, the butterflies still fluttered, but her confidence certainly grew. She knew that from the moment she walked in any door, people would begin to judge her. So from that time on, she made sure that if she wanted to give the best speech of her life, people could have no reason to write her off because of a wrinkled suit or disheveled hair. Puja is now a junior at UCLA. If you were to see her on campus dressed in sweats and her hair out of place, please don't make a judgment. Image isn't everything, it's only something.

Steve Kuo
Logan High School

Mr. Lindsey taught me one of life's most important lessons during my freshman year of high school. This was after I had lost the regional Lions Club competition—one of the most devastating losses of a very young speech career. It was especially tough after talking to Mr. Lindsey and finding out why I had lost. He told me that my preparation and content were superior to that of my competitors but I was missing one very important ingredient: poise. The seven minutes that I had spent in front of the judges while giving my speech were well received, but the twenty minutes before and after the speech were disastrous. My head was facing the floor the entire time, my legs would not stop shaking beneath the table. I looked like a nervous freshman unprepared for the event. Mr. Lindsey taught me that being a winner is not only about being ready for the moment but being poised and composed throughout the entire process. He told me, "You are judged from the moment you step into a room, and it is up to you to show poise and confidence without having to utter a single word."

Behavior is the mirror in which everyone shows their image.

—*Johann Wolfgang von Goethe*

"ONE NICE THING ABOUT BEING A CEPHALOPOD —
YOU PUT ON YOUR SHOES, YOU PUT ON YOUR
HAT AND YOU'RE DRESSED."

 AMAN GREWAL
LOGAN HIGH SCHOOL

During my four-year tenure on the James Logan Forensics Team, I competed in numerous tournaments. If anything, the one moment that I truly enjoyed was walking through a courtyard with my team. The entire lot sporting black suits, walking in a synchronized fashion, heads held up high, chests out. Not only did opposing schools know we meant business, but we looked like we meant business. Personally, I feel it is not the clothes that make the man but the man that makes the clothes. Still, I couldn't imagine engaging in some professional endeavor without a suit and tie on. It simply makes a world of difference to me. Not having much of a fashion sense in high school, I would wear the same pair of sweats three days in a row, along with my faded T-shirts. But when Saturday mornings came along, it felt as if a metamorphosis had taken place. With my hair neatly combed to the side, I would don my coat over my white shirt and red tie and go compete. Even though being a classy person does not revolve around being a well-dressed person, it helps. I always found that whenever I wore my suit, I could take on the world. The very appearance of a high school student dressed up like a lawyer, politician, or news anchor creates an image of prestige and class within not only the judge's mind but your own. It provides confidence coupled with a degree of maturity that one doesn't get wearing a T-shirt and sweats.

If you're going to show up, act like you want to be there.

—*Tim Russert*

WHEN THEY GET IT

KENDAL SLOCUM

LOGAN HIGH SCHOOL

Morehouse College graduate

I think the "aha" moment of the James Logan Forensics Team experience probably hit me subtly over the course of years rather than suddenly at any one point in time. High school was not a very enjoyable experience for me except for those few precious moments of escapism that I got from forensics tournaments.

Mr. Lindsey always said that "when you go to a job interview, they're not going to ask you how well you twirl a flag [speaking of the color guard football halftime performers], but they'll instantly recognize your professionalism." Forensics at its very core automatically teaches participants how to present themselves in a professional and confident manner. The pleasure of performing in forensics competitions is a side effect. Sometimes our educational institutions overlook the how-to-do section of citizenship for the what-to-do value of occupational knowledge. Students become saturated with definitions of what to do to be successful in society but are rarely given substantial tools on how to achieve those objectives.

My forensics experience gave me the confidence to face myself. I learned to turn away self-doubt and ward off self-loathing by recognizing that I can achieve great feats by merely being confident and believing that I can. Each of us chose different paths in life. Some of the people I went to school with have earned their Ph.D.s. Others are parents, some are teachers, legislators, soldiers, and businesspeople. We all share in common the unique period in which we participated together. At the time of this writing, the team has expanded at least fourfold in membership since I was on it, has become nationally ranked, has been politically recognized, and has been featured on "The Oprah Winfrey Show."

The success of the team can be attributed in large part to the students, but an even greater unspoken reason for the vibrant success of the program has been the coach, Mr. Tommie Lindsey, and his selfless commitment to expanding and changing the very dynamic of education through reintroducing the people perspective.

Once in a lifetime does a student come across a teacher who recognizes the specific potential in each of his or her students by making a concerted effort to get to know the student as an individual and not a statistic, race, or gender. Mr. Lindsey had a passion for teaching, and as with all great teachers, his work produced great leaders. He often referred to his students as diamonds in the rough—some because they had hard heads but mainly because he saw the beauty in us all. I have modeled my life after his compassion; I have grown from his friendship.

Aiming Above Morality

Randy

Never give up; and never, under any circumstances, no matter what—never face the facts.

—*Ruth Gordon*

When teaching transcendentalism, I show the film *Harold and Maude*. This black comedy tells the story of Harold (Bud Cort), a teenage boy obsessed with the trappings of death, and Maude (Ruth Gordon), a seventy-nine-year-old woman high on life. The eccentric Maude seems in many ways a direct descendant of Henry David Thoreau. She even quotes him without giving attribution. Attempting to teach Harold a lesson about how to "l-i-v-e," Maude says, "Aim above morality." Thoreau, as you may remember, advised, "Aim above morality. Be not simply good. Be good for something."

This lesson forms the cornerstone of my teaching philosophy. I explain to students that a true transcendentalist trusts his or her inner voice. I tell them that, contrary to popular belief, I don't need to outline a long list of rules for students to rebel against. They know the difference between right and wrong. In my class, however, doing right is not enough. Simply fulfilling expectations of correct behavior disappoints me. They must aim above morality.

Unlike other teachers who travel with students, I have had few discipline problems. In my career, I have bravely led groups of students on nearly five hundred trips. There were the occasional disagreements, of course, but no student had to make bail. I can count the violations of school rules on one hand. Admittedly, some careful planning occurs. In a room occupied by four students, for example, I place at least one student who "knows better." The key to my success, though, is not in bombarding the students with rules. We operate on the same simple rule that my grandma used with me:

Don't do anything that would disappoint me.

Thoreau could not have said it better.

DI'JONN GRIZZELL
LOGAN HIGH SCHOOL

I can remember it like it was yesterday. I was a young freshman running wild through the halls of Logan. I was out of control, and I was always in the middle of whatever was going on around campus. If there was a fight I ran toward it to see what was happening, I was the class clown in all of my classes, and I hugged up on any and every girl in my path. I didn't care how I acted—I was just having fun doing whatever. But it seemed like every time I was somewhere on campus doing something I had no business doing, Mr. Lindsey would pop up and catch me. He always told me to stay out of the way of trouble and to not go toward it. For example, he told me to walk the other way if there was a fight. He told me not to be loud and ignorant in class just to get attention and that it wasn't gentleman-like to be on every girl that I saw.

Mr. Lindsey told me that carrying myself with class is very important, because someone is always watching. Even though it took him many times to tell me these things over and over, I finally got it my senior year. When my teachers and classmates respected me for carrying myself with class and dignity unlike some of my friends, I understood what Mr. Lindsey was talking about. People noticed me for being classy and a gentleman rather than being involved in all the drama. Mr. Lindsey made me understand that there is always someone watching, waiting for you to mess up, so you must always aim higher.

A lot of people enjoy being dead. But they are not dead, really. They're just backing away from life. Reach out. Take a chance. Get hurt even. But play as well as you can. Go team, go! Give me an *L*. Give me an *I*. Give me a *V*. Give me an *E*. L-I-V-E. LIVE!

—*Maude*, Harold and Maude

JOSEPH RILEY WHITFIELD JR.
EL CERRITO HIGH SCHOOL

Mr. Lindsey forced me to embrace a higher standard of excellence that would propel me to the next stage of my development. What started off as a lesson on speechwriting, oratory, and the various forms of monologue turned into a transfer of insights on acting with integrity, seizing opportunity, and establishing a legacy. To this day, I recall our time spent deliberating on how to address my peers and their families in a way that impressed upon them the value of education as a tool to remediate ills long neglected. As a supportive audience of one, Mr. Lindsey listened to me rehearse, pointing out idiosyncrasies in my delivery and speech. His style remained both truthful and reaffirming, and as a result, I learned much about relating to my audience and using fewer words to achieve greater impact. He taught me that a complex message delivered in common language does not lose its sense of the profound.

When I delivered my speech on the night of graduation, sparks flew as I communicated the wisdom of Malcolm X and French painter Georges Seurat better than I could imagine to an audience twice the size I had expected. After I finished and the audience rose to their feet, I celebrated with a smile as Mr. Lindsey slipped away knowing that he had completed another piece of his life's work. Mr. Lindsey reached out to another young person to help him achieve his goal. I remember contemplating the value of his time with me, wondering about the source of his motivation. I know now that it was merely who he was—a person who elevates the world by believing in its young people, sharing himself with each of us and then daring us to be great.

When working on the textbook *Glencoe Speech*, the other authors and I had lengthy discussions about the teaching of ethics. No speech textbook had ever emphasized ethics in every chapter. We decided that to teach speech without talking about human conduct would be wrong. The chapter on Lincoln-Douglas debate, for example, focuses on the complexities that arise for people in all walks of life.

Students who participate in Lincoln-Douglas debate learn to draw distinctions—the difference, say, between *just* and *justify*. A person can *justify* almost any action, but that does not make the action *just*. As a student begins to grasp the need to aim above morality, the desire to know more about philosophy follows. Soon a student who may have shown little interest in school is quoting Rousseau and Plato. And suddenly Kant can. In debate lingo, that is a "turnaround that outweighs."

WHEN THEY GET IT

CHRIS DUSSEAULT

MILTON ACADEMY

Attorney

It was 1986, and I was in Kentucky. It was hard to believe and improbable for any number of reasons. Just the year before (and the year before that), I had tried out for the Milton Academy Speech and Debate Team and been rejected. Forget about winning tournaments, getting shiny trophies, and meeting girls from area high schools (not necessarily the order of importance to me at the time). I couldn't even get on our own team, let alone get to Kentucky.

But in my junior year, Randy McCutcheon's first year as coach at Milton, that all changed. I finally made the team and began to focus my efforts on Lincoln-Douglas debate. The category suited me perfectly—I got to argue with people several times a day, usually on hopelessly irresolvable topics, such as whether there is any such thing as a just war and whether it is ever justified to negotiate with terrorists (just what any seventeen-year-old boy should be thinking about). Despite my late start, I had success off the bat. I even won one of the first major tournaments in which I competed. A few months or weeks later, Randy explained that my win in that tournament had qualified me to participate in a major competition at the University of Kentucky called the Tournament of Champions, or TOC (I suppose abbreviated because Tournament of Champions is such a mouthful). I jumped at the chance, and Randy and I headed off to the Bluegrass State.

Intimidation—it is really the only word that comes to mind (well, that and *horses*, but I digress). I was a novice in the world of debate, and I was participating in a prestigious tournament limited to competitors who had won major tournaments during the course of the season. At the end of the last day of preliminary rounds, they announced that I had made the cut and was one of eight students who would advance to the quarterfinals the following day. Even more amazing, Randy informed me that I was seeded either one or two (the passage of time has obscured which) and had emerged from the preliminary rounds as one of the favorites to win the whole thing.

That night, I freaked. I needed Randy's guidance, and fast. As I peppered Randy with nervous questions, he tried his best to help and guide me. But after a while, he broke into that famous McCutcheon smile and said, "Chris, whatever is going to happen tomorrow, just remember this one thing." I waited with anticipation for the pearl of wisdom, the result of Randy's years of experience that would see me to victory over the seven young geniuses who stood in my path. And then it came: "Your sole purpose in life is to amuse me!"

What? What the heck was that? I was about to argue with some kid from Florida about whether a parliamentary form of government would be preferable to our country's current form, and all Randy could say was, "Your sole purpose in life is to amuse me"?

I was tired, I was confused, but I am pretty sure I got it even then. Randy was restoring my perspective. Randy was teaching me that while it would be great to win the tournament, and maybe I would (I didn't), we were really there to have fun. Randy was my coach, but he was also my friend. He had traveled from our school in a suburb of Boston to Lexington, Kentucky, just to coach me in a debate tournament, just to work with me. Over the course of two years together, we would travel to lots of places together, competing in lots of tournaments. We would lose some (indeed, plenty), and we would win a lot. But more important, we would have fun and we would laugh—a lot. I definitely remember our competitive successes: making the out-rounds at TOC, winning the state championship that same year, advancing relatively far in the nationals. But far more than that, I remember laughing my head off with Randy and my teammates—relishing the goofy title that Randy had bestowed on me, the Secret Debate Captain (we did not have a separate captain for debate as opposed to speech).

Life is a bit more serious now. I have a family to support—a beautiful wife, a precious son. I am a partner in a major international law firm, where I handle weighty "bet-the-company" lawsuits, report to clients and senior partners who are appropriately nervous about what is going to happen, and supervise large teams of associates, paralegals, and staff. I take my job seriously, I do everything I can to win, and we usually do. But more than occasionally, Randy's rallying cry comes to mind: "Your sole purpose in life is to amuse me!" There are times when the best thing I can do is make people smile. Make people relax. Make people laugh. Restore their perspective. I honestly believe that doing so enables us all to work harder, focus better, and win. Plus it's just a heck of a lot more fun.

MOTHER WIT

Tommie

> An ounce of mother-wit is worth a pound of school-wit.
>
> —*German proverb*

Angelica Rauch, in her paper "Saving Philosophy in Cultural Studies: The Case of Mother Wit," explains that for philosopher Immanuel Kant, "'mother wit' suggests the natural gift of forming an imaginary connection between concrete experience and abstract knowledge." In other words, the special common sense that we hope we inherit from our mothers. My grandmother, with her sixth grade education, never knew of Kant, Rousseau, or Nietzsche, but she did know of the importance of mother wit. She may never have finished high school or gone to college, but she had her Ph.D. in common sense. It's amazing the number of students I work with every day who do not have basic common sense. For example, some students spend all of their food money on clothes while we are at an away tournament. No one needs to ask them if they would like fries with that. Even a little bit of mother wit would tell them that they have to take care of the bare necessities. Beginning with food. Like eating.

Other students, however, do have mother wit—the common sense that allows them to survive not only in the school environment but also on the streets. Tafari was one of these students. High school was not a very comfortable place for him. He grew up on the streets, and he knew all of the manipulation techniques. He was a kid whose home environment was shattered by inconsistency. His parents' divorce left him empty. And at times he did things that caused him to receive negative attention.

TAFARI WALSTON

LOGAN HIGH SCHOOL

Sometimes I would cry because I didn't understand myself, and it hurt that others did not attempt to try and understand me. I was a dark-skinned African-American male trying to survive in an educational environment that feared me for my skin tone. I came into contact with Mr. Lindsey over the summer, and this was a challenge for me. I always knew that growing up on the streets can do two things to you: either kill you or make you stronger. I always felt that the street made me stronger. I always thought I had the power of intimidation. I made teachers change grades. I made kids give me their lunch money. I had girls buy me clothes. And I thought that this was it, this was the life—until I came in contact with Mr. Lindsey.

He would have none of my nonsense. Growing up in a similar situation as I, he seemed to be able to anticipate my next move, which made our relationship almost like a chess match. It was at this point that my common sense overcame everything that I'd learned on the street, and it put my power of intimidation away. I finally felt that if I was going to make it in the world, I had better stop and realize that this is someone who cared about me not because of what my skin looked like or because I could intimidate, but he cared because of what was on the inside. His caring went way beyond the call of duty.

He would definitely correct me when I was wrong. He fed me when I was hungry. In fact, when other teachers had problems with me at school, it was Mr. Lindsey who was the mediator who provided me with the sense of hope that at least somebody would hear me out—not just be on my side but actually listen. When someone takes the time to listen and to reach out, it is my responsibility to make sure that I have the common sense to appreciate what they do and then pass it on to others.

Tafari went on to take second in the country in dramatic interpretation, graduate from high school, and become active in community theater. Presently, he is involved in his church and is raising his family in southern California. One thing that he will forever retain is his ability to form an "imaginary connection between concrete experience and abstract knowledge"—his mother wit. Despite everything, Tafari had the common sense to make the right choices for the rest of his life.

PIERRE CLARK
LOGAN HIGH SCHOOL

I've always thought that having mother wit was an advantage to me. I grew up in an environment where things would be shocking to other kids but wouldn't have an effect on me. For example, to see drug dealers on the corner, prostitutes, and murders are things that for most of the kids on my team would be a shock. For me, I grew up having an extra sense to be able to know where to be and know where not to be—to know how to protect myself in such a way that I would not become involved in harmful activities. I attribute a lot of this to my grandmother and mother, who have always been my extra eyes and ears.

It's amazing how you can take mother wit and it never leaves you. When I walk in a room, I always know to look at what's around me. I know to always be aware. I know that the security guard in the store is always watching—it's not that I'd do anything but that he expects me to do something. There is the lady who pulls her purse closer to her because she thinks I am going to steal it, even though I'm dressed in a suit and on my way to a tournament. Mother wit allows me to be able to observe these kinds of things—things that surround me—and be able to react or not react. Because of this sixth sense, if you will, I can almost read the eyes of a person and tell their next move—who can be trusted and who has that fear. I've learned a lot of this by watching the eyes of that woman with the purse, the security guard, the prostitute, the drug dealer. This is what mother wit is all about to me, and it allowed me to be very successful in forensics because I had no fear of anything—not even success.

Common sense is in spite of, not as a result of, education.

—*Victor Hugo*

WHEN THEY GET IT

MICHAEL JOSHI

LOGAN HIGH SCHOOL

Harvard University student

"Disability is a matter of perception. If you can do just one thing well, you're needed by someone." If tennis player Martina Navratilova knew my mom, she might have said "*at least* one thing well." My mother has multiple sclerosis, a disease that affects the central nervous system, but there are many things she can do well. However, her disability has certainly affected the way I have grown up. Seeing her struggle to move around the house with her walker, or need a power wheelchair to go any farther, is disheartening. This is especially true because I know she used to be in a less severe stage of the disease. I see pictures or video of her when mobility was not an issue for her, and she had the energy to do what she wanted, but I do not actually remember it. Now, I more readily think of the foot brace she wears to keep herself from tripping. Unfortunately, it does not always work.

It is hard to know how to react sometimes when she falls. At first it is shocking. I dread hearing a loud crash in the house, but I dread even more seeing my mom on the floor. She is usually fine, but I can't help her up immediately, as you would normally do for someone who falls. She needs time to gather herself and summon the energy to allow herself to be picked up. It is very scary. But often I am left feeling angry. The reason she usually falls is because she was trying to do too much. Bending over to pick something up perhaps—I guess she sometimes does not realize what a bad idea it is. For some reason, I am frustrated that she was taking on more than she could handle. I mean, she should have asked someone to help her. Other times, she really does just trip; she tells herself to pick up her feet, but it is difficult. And this is so strange to me. I play sports. I have full control over my feet. I cannot fathom what it would be like to have difficulty walking. Therefore, sometimes I feel annoyed, like she was not being careful enough, but, of course this is absurd—I know it is not her fault.

On the other hand, time has allowed us to grow accustomed to the situation. In fact, she even laughs about it sometimes. She will be slow getting up out of a chair or car seat, and halfway through she will sit back down. She looks up at me, laughs, and tells me it is not funny, but she keeps laughing.

And she will never stop teasing me for this: on the basic information form of one of my college applications, I thought "Mother deceased" was "Mother diseased" (which is why there was Wite-Out over the box). After thoroughly embarrassing me and questioning if I should still apply to such a prestigious university, she could not help but find the situation comical (honestly, she knows I have no ill will toward her).

But no matter how comfortable we are with it, there are always reminders that her situation is serious. She knows people who are in a much worse stage, and we both know that there currently is no cure. And every so often, I encounter an outside perspective. My English teacher, Mr. Campbell, came to me one day and told me his sister had recently been diagnosed with MS. He talked with me about it, and I could tell that he was pretty worried. I take for granted that my mom has MS, lessening its impact on me over time. Seeing how someone else reacted made me feel almost guilty that I was not as worried about my own MS relative. Is it wrong that I have gotten used to the tangible effects her disease has? I do not mind the extra responsibilities I have around the house, and I have even accepted that the heat often made coming to my soccer games too difficult for her. And I appreciate, rather than feel sad, when people ask me how she is doing. It is nice to know that people care.

I was riding on BART to debate practice once when a lady in a wheelchair was asking for people's attention. She was shouting over the roar of the train, but I heard that she had multiple sclerosis and was on her way to the doctor without enough money for her medication. (There actually is medication for MS; it does not cure it, but my mom says it impedes its progress.) I regret to say that I do not know if I would have been able to overcome my frugal upbringing if I had not heard the words *multiple sclerosis*, but I pulled out my wallet. I found three ones and a twenty, and I knew that either way I would regret my choice: either I gave too much and should not have, or I did not give enough. Regardless, when I brought the money to the lady and told her my mother had MS, she grabbed my hand in both of hers and could not stop thanking me. I sat back down and never saw her again. I do not know if I made a difference, but I guess since I cannot help my mom, I chose to help this lady instead.

INALIENABLE WRONGS

Tommie

Don't call me irrational. You know how that
makes me crazy.

—*Niles Crane, "Frasier"*

S ome students never have an unexpressed thought. Their belief
in unlimited freedom of expression is enough to drive a ratio-
nal person crazy. Is it any wonder that America's Declaration of
Independence still haunts me? Supposedly, we are endowed with
certain inalienable rights, including life, liberty, and the pursuit
of happiness.

Unfortunately, students often have a different interpretation,
a selfish one. I once had a student on the team who did not do
well at tournaments. She was a student who should have been
doing oratory instead of dramatic interpretation, but she wanted
to pursue dramatic interp because she thought she was the next

Halle Berry. It didn't matter what selection was recommended for her to perform, it was never good enough. Finally, we got to the point that there was discussion where she said to me that she hated being on the team and hated me as her coach. My response: she should leave the team immediately. She stated, "I'm not leaving this program. I have a right to be on this team."

In what I believed to be a very calm manner, I let her know that no one has that right. It is a privilege to participate in the program. Participating in the program was not enumerated in any of our country's founding documents, even though in her moment of inanity, she might have thought so. Soon after our conversation, the student did quit the team. I, shocked by the student's response, phoned Randy to relay my disbelief, and he shared a story with me about a student who charged into his office and demanded that he listen to her give a speech. Randy replied that she would have to wait until he finished working with another team member. The student's response was, "You have to listen to me right now. I pay your salary."

NICHOLAS PARRILLA
LOGAN HIGH SCHOOL

I remember Mr. Lindsey getting that phone call from back home (Room 408). Bonan, the little know-it-all boy on the team, was verbally slapped by some girl at school for his incessant back talk. Of course, my first emotion was joy when I heard the news, considering he tried to mock me in class one day and also threw a hanger, which barely missed my beautiful face. He not only disrespected his teammates, but many of us on the team felt that he disrespected Mr. Lindsey by constantly debating his decisions, which hurt me deeply. A number of us felt he was most deserving of what happened to him.

Then I was sitting at the table with Mr. Lindsey and Mr. Marks as they both were discussing Bonan's explicit mind and how no one understands what he goes through. I thought about how his mind is overdeveloped for his body and how he must feel like he needs to show some strength over others to prove himself capable of being his own individual. As the subject changed, I was still thinking about how he must feel when he is constantly trying to prove himself as a strong individual. That's when I understood. I learned that people put layers on their true personality to show others what they want them to see and also to disguise weaknesses. What I saw in my teammate Bonan was not a weakness but more the desire to be accepted as one of us regardless of his exceptions and differences, which I had finally realized wasn't so very different from how I felt.

One of the big themes of the team in 2005 was celebrating the different personalities and characters. I realized that there is nothing wrong with being different as long as a person can remain tasteful, generous, disciplined, and good-hearted. People get better responses from other people when they search for the sincerity. Accordingly, when Bonan joined us the next day in Atlanta, I made a point to be much nicer to him and embrace him as a teammate—and I got a better response from him. The more he noticed my kinder approach to him, the more he engaged in conversation with me. I finally got the response that I wanted from Bonan. All because I respected him, and he, in turn, respected me.

Another example of an inalienable wrong occurred at a national tournament. Two of my students were at odds. One of the students came to me and demanded that the other be eliminated from the team or else she would quit. I had to explain to that student that the only right that she had was her option to quit, not to tell me who else should be dismissed from the team. This feud continued for months. There were some hard feelings and much bitterness; however, I had to make the decision that I thought would be the best for the team. I remember expressing to her mother and father that it is a privilege to be in our program and that no student has the right to determine who is going to be on or off this team.

The final example involves another student who qualified for the national tournament. Neither his mother nor his father had the time to take him to the airport to get to the tournament or the money to pay for his flight. I ended up paying for him. The young man did extremely well at the tournament, and when he returned, his family never came to pick him up. I had to make the arrangements for his ride home. After about three weeks, I received a phone call from his mother, demanding that he receive some financial compensation for doing well at the tournament. I explained to her at the time that there were copyright laws involved, and using an author's script precluded getting any monetary compensation. She yelled at me, then cursed me, and said she would pursue this matter in court. Needless to say, the legal threats were not pursued.

In all of these cases, we have found people who obviously misinterpreted the intent of the framers of the Declaration of Independence or in some inexplicable way confused inalienable rights with inalienable wrongs. They felt that they were owed something that they didn't rightfully earn. After these incidents, I opted to draw my own charter, to grant my students appropriate rights and responsibilities. They had the right to participate, to be a part of this program, and to learn what good sportsmanship was about. And, most important, they had the responsibility to care about others more than themselves.

WHEN THEY GET IT

BONAN ZHOU

LOGAN HIGH SCHOOL

After reading Bonan's interpretation of "When They Get It," I had to ask myself if I'd ever thrown scissors or a stapler at anyone or executed a dropkick. But it's obvious that Bonan can make you believe that anything is possible. In fact, it doesn't even sound like a bad idea.

Dear Mr. Lindsey,

I'll never forget the day when you drop-kicked a student. You heard me. I've seen you throw scissors, staplers, and other office supplies, but drop-kick? No, impossible. Men of your proportions were not meant to launch human projectiles.

But one day, returning from one of my routine trips to the cafeteria, I saw a student run out the doors of Room 408, and as I entered the room, dozens of students with jaws dropped stared at you as you walked back into your office. I soon discovered that a dropkick had, indeed, occurred. Missing that spectacle was one of the saddest moments of my life. My seventy-five-cent cookie and microwave burrito tasted even worse than they normally did because every bite was a reminder of your dropkick, a dropkick that I'd probably never again see.

Like many other high school students, I had a short attention span, so I had already forgotten about the incident by eighth period. During the debate meeting after school, I didn't even feel scared about not doing my homework, since the debate coaches never really checked anyway (don't tell them I said that).

The next day, in the middle of class, you called me into your office. At first, I thought I had heard wrong, that you were calling some other student. But then it dawned on me. No one else's name sounds even remotely like Bonan Zhou.

I slowly opened your office door. Then you looked up from your desk. And you told me that I hadn't been turning in my debate assignments. How did you know? The debate coaches didn't keep a record of our work! "Oh my God," I thought, "it's my turn to get drop-kicked. Wait. What did you just say? I can go?" At first I thought it was a trick, but then I realized that for some reason, you had shown me mercy. I emerged from the office unscathed.

And that, Mr. Lindsey, was better than witnessing all the drop-kicks in the world.

Some Things Stay the Same

Tommie

> The time is always right to do right.
>
> —*Martin Luther King Jr.*

The civil rights movement was a very challenging time for our country. I personally can remember people giving their lives for the voting rights of African-American people in the South. I can remember Dick Gregory, Martin Luther King Jr., and Fannie Lou Hamer. I remember watching the dogs on the television attacking people, the water hoses, and the hatred that was in the visage of racist Americans who felt it was not fair for African-Americans even to eat in all-white restaurants. What a sacrifice for equality. Through the observations of Cherie, you will see that, unfortunately, things have not changed enough.

CHERIE JOHNSON
LOGAN HIGH SCHOOL

I remember watching videos that Mr. Lindsey showed in class about the civil rights movement and people wanting to eat in a restaurant where they typically were refused service. The Jim Crow laws were something that were pretty fresh in my mind, but coming from a small town that was very diverse, I could never have imagined that such a situation ever existed. Refusing anyone service because of their race just wasn't something that I could believe.

In my sophomore year, we traveled to Chicago; it was a long plane ride but a pleasant trip. The reason being, there were fifteen of us who were headed to a forensics tournament, and we all seemed to get along very well, as is typical of our team. We checked in at the hotel and put our bags in our rooms. I remember Mr. Lindsey taking us to a restaurant to eat. We sat there in the restaurant for about forty minutes, and no one provided service. Then Mr. Lindsey asked if we were going to be served. We sat there for another fifteen minutes, and still, no one had come to take our orders.

I looked into the faces of my teammates and we were all confused. We had never dealt with this kind of treatment before and therefore did not know how to react. Mr. Lindsey asked us to get up and walk toward the van. We found another place to eat that evening. However, my spirits were down because this was in 2001, and who would have thought that the feeling that those people had during the civil rights movement would be something that I would have to feel?

I remember a statement by Martin Luther King Jr. He said he had been to a number of places all over the South but had never seen racism like what he experienced in some neighborhoods of Chicago. I kept seeing that restaurant in my mind all evening. I didn't rest well that night. I tried to focus on my performance to keep my mind away from such a negative experience.

I know Mr. Lindsey felt my pain. He didn't say anything about it, but he showed it with his actions. The next night, he took us to the south side of Chicago and we ate at this soul food restaurant, and the service that we got was something incredible. The food was great, the company was fantastic, and most important, my spirits were uplifted. However, this situation will forever stay in my mind. It showed me that I had more in common with those people who tried to eat at a restaurant during the civil rights movement than I thought. It always goes to show you some things never change—they stay the same.

It demands great spiritual resilience not to hate the hater whose foot is on your neck, and an even greater miracle of perception and charity not to teach your child to hate.

—*James Baldwin*

PAUL BALDO
LOGAN HIGH SCHOOL

The lessons learned in the classroom should always be with you. If a teacher is effective, class will never be dismissed for a student. A teacher's level of excellence and impact is judged on the longevity of that teacher's message. A great lesson I learned from my parents, which was reinforced by Mr. Lindsey, was how to behave with class. According to my parents and Mr. Lindsey, classy people are those who determine their own human worth and express that worth through every action. They define themselves and do not allow others to determine who they are. During my four years in Mr. Lindsey's class, I learned that people who stand in genuine confidence are those who know their human worth. They are humble in victory and gracious in defeat, and they never allow anyone to use them as a doormat.

Determining one's worth is vital to living a classy life. There are things in life that never change. Racism, prejudice, and discrimination—the insidious cancers that continue to pervade our lives—have affected my life in innumerable ways. I joined speech and debate because I wanted to speak well and not be judged because of an accent. I have been in many situations where I have felt looked down upon because of the color of my skin. However, participating in forensics has not been the easiest road traveled by our team. We are a team dominated by minorities and have been treated horribly by some teams and those threatened by the success of high school students from "nontraditional" backgrounds.

During a tournament at the University of Southern California, a debater made one of my teammates—our top debater with three California state championships under her belt—cry because he did not appreciate an African-American woman winning the round. Also, a restaurant in Chicago refused to serve our team. However, even after all of this maltreatment, our team has stood tall in confidence and continues to do so because we know our worth. A number of teammates confronted the debater and made him apologize, and after realizing the racist intentions of the restaurant, Mr. Lindsey confronted the manager and his staff. We walked out with our dignity. Mr. Lindsey's classiness puts him in a class all his own. Through Mr. Lindsey's example, I have been able to live a classy life. I can admit when I am wrong, but I can also stand tall with my head up and confront someone when they are incorrect. For me, Mr. Lindsey's class is never dismissed because I am always confronted by situations that require looking back at the lessons learned in Room 408 for guidance.

You must be the change you wish to see in the world.

—*Mohandas Gandhi*

When They Get It

Kelly Metters

Logan High School

University of San Francisco Law School student

I remember Mr. Lindsey standing in front of our class and telling us about an incident that had taken place during the past weekend. He had offered to carry a bag for a woman who was struggling to make it to her car. In response to his courtesy, she asked him, "Oh, are you the janitor?" Our class sighed, frustrated. Nobody gasped with shock or dismay; we had heard many stories like this one. Mr. Lindsey continued, "I had to educate her. I said, 'No, I'm actually the director of forensics here at James Logan High School.'"

Mr. Lindsey taught us that you have to just educate people, but without being rude or lashing out. It seemed to me then that Mr. Lindsey always had to educate someone. During the forensics rounds, ballots were sometimes returned with a judge's comment, "Good job! But did you write this yourself?" Outside the forensics rounds, the presumptions were more disheartening. On one occasion at an invitational, I remember peering out of an upstairs hotel window and seeing a teammate in handcuffs—mistaken identity. Mr. Lindsey handled the whole gamut the same, with poise. Whether it was confronting a judge who was in error or explaining to police officers that they had mistaken one of our kids for an armed robbery suspect, Mr. Lindsey handled these situations in the same manner he expected us to conduct ourselves as a team, with class. During my junior year in high school, I began to "get it." His repetitive mantras, "conduct yourselves as champions," "with class," and "educate people," began to sink in.

There was a state preliminary round where the congress topic was on using primarily "third-world" nations as test subjects for experimental HIV/AIDS medication. I remember being so appalled at one of the competitor's bigoted, ethnocentric statements about why "these people" were worth the sacrifice that I confronted her as inappropriate during cross-examination. I asked why the greater good had to come at the expense of the less fortunate and further addressed "abuses of privilege" in my speech. After the round another competitor said she appreciated my questions in the round and the types of issues I raised.

It was clear to me then that Mr. Lindsey was teaching me a skill that was necessary to be successful well beyond the final round of state; he was teaching me, teaching us all, the appropriate way to confront and combat ignorance. Forensics was cultivating my ability to speak up and was building my confidence in my own unique voice. I greatly valued (and *still* appreciate) the by-product of Mr. Lindsey's energy and the forensics program; they gave me the ability to educate my peers and judges inside of the forensics rounds and to correct misjudgments of individuals outside of the forensics rounds, with poise, with class.

Heart Breaks

Tommie

The world is not respectable; it is mortal, tormented, confused, deluded forever; but it is shot through with beauty, with love, with glints of courage and laughter; and in these, the spirit blooms.

—*George Santayana*

The spirit blooms where it is nurtured. Unfortunately, most people believe that students being detained in a juvenile facility will never bloom. That, for these students, a work ethic is an illusion or, even worse, an aberration. But that was not my belief. I knew it was challenging for them to focus on academics rather than their prison sentences. And teaching in a self-contained classroom with kids who were detained for murder, rape, and many other nefarious crimes was a challenge for me as well. But somehow, even though my students were going through intense difficulties and adjustments in life, I would always try to give them something extra, to reach their hearts, minds, and souls.

I decided to institute a Christmas speech contest, instructing the students to speak on what the holidays meant to them. I vividly remember an interaction that took place on the day of the first contest. One of my students from a broken home looked at me and said, "This is the first time anybody has done anything for me at Christmas."

The competition was so successful that I decided to try a Martin Luther King Jr. speech contest. I felt that Dr. King's birthday was more often perceived as a day off than a day of celebration. When I brought this idea to the powers that be, they rejected it. After all, these students were in jail to be punished, not rewarded. I could have chosen to walk away and be just one more adult abandoning these kids. Instead, I was able to convince one of the head counselors in Unit D to allow us to hold the contest anyway. I was astonished by the students' efforts at speechmaking and marveled at their ability to express themselves in a constructive way as they delivered the speeches on their dreams.

But all students face heartbreaks, whether they are in a juvenile detention facility or not. Each student must choose to face the world with "glints of courage and laughter." Eric, a student I had years later, understood this very well.

ERIC FOGEL
LOGAN HIGH SCHOOL

At the end of my second year in law school, I noticed a large, swollen bump in my mouth. At first I didn't pay it any attention. But it grew larger and larger. When I started having trouble speaking, I went in to have it checked. The diagnosis was cancer, and I was immediately put on chemotherapy and radiation treatment. I lost all my hair. I lost all my taste. I lost all my energy. There was a time when I was just living on the floor.

Never once did I let it bring me down. I think the doctors and everybody thought I was in denial or something. When the doctors first told me that I had cancer, they looked more uncomfortable than me. I actually felt obligated to put them at ease! I remember one doctor walking away and whispering to another that he had never seen anybody take it so well.

It didn't bother me because I had learned from Mr. Lindsey that life is not a matter of winning or losing, or how long or short you have on this planet, or how rich or poor you are. Life is about finding your passion.

As I began to work through the juvenile system, I found some kids whose lives I couldn't change. Sadly, though, I came to the realization that sometimes these students were not able to get themselves out of the penal system, and that was the biggest heartbreak of all. However, what they will always remember is the plaque that hung over Unit D—a plaque that bore Martin Luther King Jr.'s name alongside the winners of our speech contests. Having listened to those student speakers, I hope they will learn that it is when people expect the least from you that you can be at your best. As Dr. King said, "The ultimate measure of a [person] is not where [he or she] stands in moments of comfort and convenience, but where [he or she] stands at times of challenge and controversy."

WHEN THEY GET IT

JAMIE WALKER

LOGAN HIGH SCHOOL

*Noted journalist, literary activist, and author
of* Signifyin' Me: New and Selected Poems

Mr. Lindsey didn't know it at the time, but when I planned to join the Drama Department during my first year at James Logan High School, I was joining because I not only imagined that I'd one day become an award-winning, accomplished actress, but I also secretly hoped to "reclaim" my speaking voice after surviving years of childhood sexual abuse. No one knew my personal history at the time. I was popular around campus, but deep inside I was very shy, yearning for creative and artistic expression. I was yearning to use my own voice and talents so that I might one day touch and inspire others.

And somehow even then Mr. Lindsey saw it in me, this young black girl from Oakland, California, longing to give a name to the nameless and a face to the faceless. He encouraged me to join the forensics team instead of the Drama Department because he saw something in me. And although I was deeply crushed because I thought I would never again be able to perform onstage when he dragged me (almost literally—but quite humorously) away from the Drama Department and into his forensics classroom on the first day of school, what I learned in Mr. Lindsey's class would exceed all of my greatest expectations.

He sharpened my eye for selecting outstanding monologues with literary value. He helped me to hone and perfect my craft, as well as to explore the depth, impact, and range of my speaking voice. Mr. Lindsey introduced me to the plays of August Wilson and Ntozake Shange and nurtured my love for both Maya Angelou's and Nikki Giovanni's poetry. He showed me a host of awards that he knew I'd one day own and sat me down in front of a television with a VCR, to study public speaking techniques. Mr. Lindsey took me all over the country—not just to compete, but to share the amazing gift that God had given me with the world. Under his tutelage, I became a symbolic conveyor of words and oral histories—resonant with the beauty and secrets of my ancient ancestral past.

I didn't know it then, but he was immersing me in my own literary tradition—that is, a black woman's literary tradition comprising a fierce legacy of struggle and culture of resistance. On Mr. Lindsey's team, I developed integrity and learned the power of both the spoken and written word. With his keen eye for matching students and their skills with selected plays by well-known authors, I learned to articulate black women's silences through characters like Rose from August Wilson's play *Fences* and also through such poems as "Still I Rise" by Maya Angelou and "Ego Trippin'" by Nikki Giovanni.

I think I got it toward the end of my first year on his team when I won the school's first state championship in dramatic interpretation. I got it when I realized that my performances could bring tears to the members of my audience—young and old alike— regardless of race, gender, creed, or class. I got it when I was asked (years later) to serve on literary panels with renowned artists like Sonia Sanchez, Amiri Baraka, and Toni Morrison. I got it when I eventually met August Wilson in person (while I was in graduate school at Howard University) and when my feature stories began gracing the cover of the *New York Amsterdam News*, *San Francisco Bay View*, and *Tennessee Tribune*.

I got it when Camille O. Cosby (wife of Bill Cosby) and journalist Renee Poussaint asked me to follow Phylicia Rashad at the Kennedy Center in Washington, D.C., in introducing historic "visionary elders" like the late Ray Charles, the late Ossie Davis, Ruby Dee, and Jimmy Heath.

But most of all, I got it on the day that I first met Mr. Lindsey—when he saw that first spark in my eyes as I desperately tried to join the drama team. It was then that he taught me that my given circumstances could never hold me back—that deep within me lay unlimited power and possibilities. Mr. Lindsey taught me that to gain control over my speaking voice was truly an act of freedom. No longer mute, or as timid or shy as I was in the past, I have since committed myself to becoming a collector of words and oral histories. I am now a bearer and keeper of our own traditions, writing like the many authors Mr. Lindsey introduced me to in his class. And for this—for his leadership, service, and mentoring—I am ever so grateful.

SWALLOWING PRIDE

Randy

I'm going to say this with all the humility I can
summon up. I'm the greatest trial lawyer that
ever lived.

—*Denny Crane, "Boston Legal"*

I could be wrong, [an excruciatingly long pause]
but I'm not.

—*Adrian Monk, "Monk"*

Television may not be the best place for students to learn about
humility. The lead characters on successful television shows
seem, for the most part, to be prideful. Occasionally, though,

someone appears on the telly with the right spirit. Consider Morgan Freeman, who won the Oscar for best supporting actor for his role as a sagelike ex-prizefighter in *Million Dollar Baby*. Freeman covered his bases by saying, "I want to thank everybody I ever met."

Humility, of course, is more than thanking everyone. Students must learn that humility is a virtue. I try to help them understand that (1) they should do the best they can without the need for recognition and (2) they must treat everyone with respect. One of my most disappointing experiences as a speech coach was hearing a student of mine taunt students from another team after those students lost a round. My student had already qualified to compete at the national tournament. I promptly removed her from the team. No trip to nationals that she had fought so hard to earn. Years later, that same student nominated me for a Coaches' Hall of Fame honor. Lessons sometimes come hard, but they do come.

I remember reading the transcript of an interview with George Gershwin. A reporter asked him how long it had taken him to write *Rhapsody in Blue*. Gershwin replied, "All of my life." He was not only recognizing that any individual is the sum of all of his or her life experiences but was, at the same time, honoring everyone who had influenced him along the way.

Honor and humility. Always the right notes to play.

 MIRIAM NALAMUNSI
LOGAN HIGH SCHOOL

I couldn't believe it.

I searched the face of the man who was talking, hoping that maybe there was some mistake. But he finished his announcement, and none of the other judges said anything. It was done.

"I DON'T HAVE THE TEST I SCHEDULED FOR TODAY. MY DOG ATE IT."

This final debate round had been delayed, so we were given our respective trophies on the spot. Extending my hand, I turned to my opponent. "Congratulations," I said, a wide smile plastered on my face. He was a friend of mine, so I even gave him a hug. Tears of disappointment and frustration started welling up in my eyes, so I gathered my papers and all but ran out the door.

I just couldn't believe it.

Some rounds were a toss-up; you had no idea which way the judges would vote. Other rounds you thought you knew who won, but you could understand if the judges voted the other way. Then there were rounds that were slam dunks. All competitors know that feeling—the feeling of a job well done, a feat perfectly executed with victory served on a silver platter. I had felt all those things, and yet I had lost. I recalled a book I was reading where the protagonist insisted that second place was just the first-place loser. "That is what I am today," I thought bitterly to myself, "a first-place loser."

"Miriam," I heard my opponent yell out.

I couldn't muster the energy to smile this time, so as I turned to face him, I just said, "Wuzup?" in a voice as tired as I felt. My eyes grazed over his trophy, but I quickly looked away, silently chanting to myself, "You will not cry. You will not cry."

"You deserve this one," he said, offering me his first-place trophy. "We both know you won that round."

"Wouldn't that be funny if competitors judged their own rounds?" I said, a chuckle masking the sudden weakness I felt inside. "But that is what judges are for, and they said it was your round. Congratulations, really. First place is yours." I hugged him again before walking away.

As my opponent was offering me his trophy, I could hear Mr. Lindsey's voice admonishing us that being a member of our team meant adhering to a high standard of behavior, in our rounds and out of our rounds, whether we won or lost. When I entered the competition, I agreed to the rules of the game, and by those rules, my opponent had earned the first-place trophy. As I walked away this time, the tears didn't come back because I finally understood what Mr. Lindsey had always told us: even champions don't win all the time.

Pride makes us artificial and humility makes us real.

—*Thomas Merton*

WHEN THEY GET IT

NICOLE DAYAO OCAMPO

LOGAN HIGH SCHOOL

University of California, Davis, student

Being in Mr. Lindsey's forensics class, I'm surprised I didn't develop an ulcer. It's not that Mr. Lindsey was terribly ruthless to his students or was always ornery and short-tempered—in fact, he was quite the opposite. He was overwhelmingly patient with students who even I felt were out of line, and he always took the time to hear the class's views on controversial issues. What made Mr. Lindsey so intimidating was that everyone knew he was one of those teachers who demanded respect without a single word or action coming from him. There was almost a type of reverence when the upperclassmen spoke of him to the underclassmen, indicating that we should never take what we say to him or about him lightly. They built him up to be of almost mythic proportions. So when I was called into his office—the one we always peered into but could never enter without permission—it threw my heart into unhealthy palpitations.

He began speaking. I stood there nervously, occasionally casting my eyes downward, afraid to look him in the eyes. The reason he called me in was to discuss my spot for the Long Beach tournament and how he was sorry but he would have to give it to an upperclassman instead. I had absolutely no problem with that, and I understood the reasons for his decision. I responded, "That's OK, Mr. Lindsey, and thank you for the opportunity to go."

At the time, I didn't think much of what I had said, but Mr. Lindsey paused for a moment and looked up from his paperwork to tell me, "Don't worry, you'll have many more opportunities in the future to compete, I'm sure." And with that I turned to exit the office, a little confused and mostly relieved.

It took a few seconds to sink in, but it was probably at that moment when I realized the importance of what I was a part of. This was a place where effort, gratitude, and respect would lead me to bigger and greater successes, where it was OK to be mature and strive for something better. I no longer felt like "just another freshman" but like a student who had four years to make some sort of difference in the forensics world and the rest of my life to impact the entire world. I didn't have to wait for the opportunities to come along; I was the one who could create my own destiny. For the four years following that moment, Mr. Lindsey nurtured this attitude and helped to develop a confidence that will carry me throughout life. Sure, he taught me the basics of good speaking and presentation, but it's these personal lessons that demystified the myth and made real the sincerity of the man.

"GOT IDEA. TALK BETTER. COMBINE WORDS. MAKE SENTENCES."

THE THIRD TRUTH

WORDS SELDOM FAIL YOU

Words Seldom Fail You

Randy

You can stroke people with words.

—*F. Scott Fitzgerald*

I n an interview with Lesley Stahl, Bill Maher observed that the reason for the lasting popularity of "60 Minutes" was the show's success in "making interesting what is important." As teachers, we are not very good at that. Too often we fail to help students discern what really matters. Then we present our daily hodgepodge in an uninteresting way. And we wonder why so many students don't tune in.

Students learn from us that words matter. That is, if we make the process of learning those words joyful. Modeling imaginative language use is our responsibility as teachers. Students need to see us struggle for what Emily Dickinson called the "chiefest word, the best word." Our struggle and our joy free them. The creative teacher gives students permission to explore their own imaginations.

Too many teachers trivialize content by relying on what I call a "PowerPoint presentation" approach in the classroom. The information these teachers present is clear and accurate. But the way they use language fails to engage students. My favorite example of such an approach is Peter Norvig's "PowerPoint Gettysburg Address." Norvig reduces the eloquence of Abraham Lincoln to bulleted phrases that demean this historic occasion.

Agenda
• Met on battlefield (great)
• Dedicate portion of field—fitting!
• Unfinished work (great tasks)

We must continually remind students of the importance of words. If we don't, classroom presentations will resemble what Edward R. Tufte compares to a school play: "very loud, very slow, and very simple." Words seldom fail you. You may fail them, though.

I remember hearing of an English professor who, after concluding the study of Herman Melville's novel *Moby Dick*, asked the students to "draw it." In this exercise, the student is forced to "see" what the words mean. That's a far cry from fishing in their memories for an answer to a factual question, such as this: in the opening sentence of Melville's novel, who says, "Call me"? A student's response to such questions is likely to be the Jimmy Buffett refrain "If the phone doesn't ring, it's me."

Let me explain what I mean. Here's an exercise that encourages students to use words in an imaginative way. When teaching John Guare's *Six Degrees of Separation*, I want students to experience the creative writing process. I first ask them to study this brief excerpt from the play:

I read somewhere that everybody on this planet is separated by only six other people. Six degrees of separation. Between us and everybody else on this planet. The President of the United States. A gondolier in Venice. Fill in the names. I find that (A) tremendously comforting that we're so close and (B) like Chinese water torture that we're so close. Because you have to find the right six people to make the connection. It's not just big names. It's anyone. A native in the rain forest. A Tierra del Fuegan. An Eskimo. I am bound to everyone on this planet by a trail of six people. . . . But to find the right six people.

I then challenge the students to write and to deliver their own brief monologues. The monologue should reveal the "right six people" and how they found them. I explain to the students that they have to create six imaginary characters with a connection to each other and eventually to them. Intrigued by the possibilities, students produce remarkable monologues. Forget Tierra del Fuegans. Reporters from Reuters, tsunami exploiters, and surgeons slicing goiters people my classroom. On the other hand, I could settle for asking them to name the characters who appear in Act II of Guare's play.

Remember: this truth is not merely about the words used by teachers. The value of students mastering written and oral communication skills cannot be overstated. Teachers make such mastery "popular." Admittedly, we are not the producers of "60 Minutes." We are teachers. But the clock is still ticking.

WORD MEETINGS

Tommie

Education is our passport to the future, for tomorrow belongs to the people who prepare for it today.

—*Malcolm X*

Malcolm X, in his autobiography, shares with us what impact words had on his life. Frustrated by his inability to write a letter, he began to read the dictionary one page at a time. He writes, "During my time in prison, I guess I learned a million words." As Malcolm's word base broadened, so did his curiosity for knowledge. I believe learning words and their meanings allows students to grow far beyond their expectations. Therefore, I stress vocabulary development in my classes. Understanding words frees the mind of a child from ignorance. In Jeff Stetson's play *The Meeting*, the words of the playwright empower my students. The play received a number of drama awards for its intriguing idea of what would have happened if Martin Luther King Jr. and Malcolm X had met to discuss their respective approaches to dealing with racism in our society. (In truth, the two men did meet in their lifetimes but only for about twenty seconds.) As my students begin to read the play, I observe the words on the page affecting them, leaving to the imagination what might have occurred. Through reading and listening to the words of the play, my students become a part of history. Robert and Pierre, two of my former students who performed *The Meeting*, were absorbed by the words of Martin Luther King and Malcolm X, words that challenged them to think of what might have been:

> **MLK:** Malcolm, do you think that we could've changed history?
> **Malcolm X:** If we only had time . . . if we only had time.

This exchange between Martin and Malcolm toward the end of the play allowed Robert and Pierre to understand that people can have different views and still find a common place. Needless to say, Robert and Pierre were both strengthened by the words that might have brought two powerful leaders together. As my colleague Randy has said to both his students and mine, communication does matter.

I am always careful in assigning *The Meeting* to particular kinds of students: students who are in need of hope and direction—kids who need words to provide encouragement and direction in their lives.

Sam Ransom, a former student of mine who played football for the Air Force Academy, recently completed his master's degree in business at Loyola Marymount. Sam was my first student to qualify for nationals. He explains the importance of words to him.

SAM RANSOM
LOGAN HIGH SCHOOL

In forensics I used to love having the audience in the palm of my hand, hanging on my next word. I enjoyed taking them along my verbal journey, confident that in the end, we would be seeing eye to eye. While the delivery was important, the words were paramount! I learned that the summers spent researching and thumbing through the thesaurus for that one perfect word were like gold when standing in front of an audience. Whether it was laughing about our society's lust for physical beauty or brooding over our obligations to give back and improve this society, my words, not my delivery, were the real hooks.

Are words more powerful than a gun? Without a doubt! Words can destroy a dream, murder an imagination, and devour a future. Used properly, and fueled by an honest and compassionate heart, words can inspire greatness beyond measure. In America we champion our right to free speech, yet we lament the negative effects that so much free access to unsavory speech has on our society. For these reasons, I have placed a very high standard on the words I choose. When someone is angered by something I did, I don't dismiss it—I acknowledge my mistake and seek forgiveness. When someone wants to bait me into an argument, I don't accept the invitation by spewing expletives—I defuse the situation with kindness and logic. When a young man asks me, "Why do you believe in Jesus?" I don't say, "Because everyone does"—I take the time to explain to him how Jesus loved us so much that he suffered unimaginably to give us sinners a chance to enter heaven. The words I select have the power to make someone's day brighter, to solve someone's problem, or to change someone's life. Such awesome ability to affect others is far too important to take cavalierly.

Booker T. Washington wrote, "Through the power of words and actions, we make people stronger or weaker. We lift people up, or we drag them down." My hope is that all of my students were at some time lifted.

WHEN THEY GET IT

MICHAEL JOSHI

LOGAN HIGH SCHOOL

Harvard University student

My first year with the James Logan Forensics Team passed uneventfully, as I was relatively uninvolved with the two-hundred-plus-student program. This may have had something to do with my unfamiliarity with the head coach, Mr. Tommie Lindsey, who I felt was intimidating and unapproachable. However, early my sophomore year, Mr. Lindsey discovered there was this young kid called Mike who was terrified of him (to this day, I maintain that *terrified* was too strong a word). Well, he confronted me about this at CSU Long Beach's annual high school speech tournament, right before my final round of congress. He said he'd heard I was afraid of him—and has since claimed that I didn't respond (I guess my words were meeting elsewhere that day). "Well," he said then, "I tell you what: I'll buy you dinner if you win your round." Later that evening (after a two-hour round and a gut-wrenching awards ceremony), I reluctantly paid for my own dinner. But on the bright side, I hadn't made a fool of myself by being unable to say a single word in front of my hard-to-please speech coach—all right, so maybe it was not what I had hoped.

So why are words so important? Why did one professor at Cal State Hayward keep track of the vocabulary my teammate and I used during a presentation, proceeding to read them to her students after we'd finished? Some argue we should be more concerned with sticks and stones but forget the powerful meanings that words can own. For this reason, both those who use words and those who listen must consider that words can carry hidden meanings for certain people. I learned this lesson the hard way. Last year at the Barkley Forum (a tournament hosted by Emory University in Atlanta, Georgia), I lost my sixth and final preliminary round and ended up not advancing to elimination rounds. My judge told me after the round that he had voted against me because during the debate, I had based my position on a theory of international relations that he happened to hate. Judges are supposed to be neutral, and I was already upset that my judge had allowed his personal opinions to affect his decision. However, at that time, I didn't know the extent to which he'd intervened.

While waiting for our plane to depart at the airport, Mr. Lindsey let us see our ballots from the tournament. I found my sixth-round ballot and almost exploded. My judge had labeled me "morally repugnant" and had given me the lowest number of speaker points the ballot would allow. Speaker points are a measure of your skill as a speaker, so you could potentially lose a round and still have higher speaker points than your opponent. These points are important because they delineate ranks for debaters with the same record. He said he gave me low speaks to prevent me from "spewing this stuff in later rounds," which was arguably an unjustified abuse of his power. I discovered that my win-loss record was good enough for me to advance to elimination rounds but that my offended judge had succeeded: my cumulative speaker points unfortunately seeded me too low. One judge had unilaterally prevented me from advancing, all because I had said one word.

Mr. Lindsey has expressed the importance of using communication to inspire and teach, but we are often reminded, through competition or exposure to certain materials, that words can also be hateful and offensive. Everyone is entitled to his or her own perspective, implying that words inevitably are forced to confront the biases of their listeners. My experience has taught me that the key is making these meetings conciliatory. Whereas speakers must heed the significance of the meaning associated with their words, listeners must be respectful and wary of harshly interpreting the expression of others. Too often, the predicaments we face are the consequence of rash judgments. We forget that when speakers and their words meet listeners and their ears, it takes time for each party to truly understand the other.

PRACTICAL MATTERS

MEETING OF MINDS

"**M**eeting of Minds," created by Steve Allen, was hailed by one critic as "the ultimate talk show." This PBS program conformed to the typical talk show format but with a twist. The featured guests played significant roles in history. Try to imagine Cleopatra interacting with Attila the Hun. Or Charles Darwin. Or Thomas Jefferson. Well, Allen did. And the viewing audience was the better for these mind melds.

Students, too, benefit by creating these imaginary conversations. The key is to encourage extensive and careful research. The observations of each character should be based on truth. A creative teacher will choose characters that capture students' imaginations. Say, Jose Canseco, Babe Ruth, and Hippocrates discussing the legitimacy of steroid use. Or perhaps George W. Bush, Marie Antoinette, and Albert Camus discussing capital punishment. If teachers select their talk show guests wisely, this exercise decreases historical illiteracy as it increases familiarity with the great thinkers of the past.

The what-if premise behind this program can be applied in other ways. For example, I encourage my speech students to participate in National History Day, a yearlong education program that culminates in a national contest each June. The students enter the individual and group "performance" categories. One year five of my students won an all-expenses-paid trip to Greece. They performed my original play *Agora-met's Delight* (the title was taken, as you might have guessed, from the name of the Greek marketplace).

The play was based on a what-if scenario. What would have happened if a franchiser from today was transported back in time to the agora? And what if this franchiser tried to convince two Greek brothers to franchise their olive stands throughout Greece? Two students portrayed the Greek chorus to provide the necessary exposition. The clash between economic systems and the merging of modern drama with Greek drama heightened the interest of the judges. And we added as much humor as possible.

What-if scenarios intrigue students. With some imagination, they can be used for classroom assignments, application essays, and scholarship contests.

> What is supposed to be true education is, for millions, a sort of comedy of errors.
> —*Steve Allen, from the Foreword to* Get Off My Brain

THE "BOB" FACTOR

Randy

When my time comes, just skin me and put me up there on Trigger, just as though nothing had changed.

—*Roy Rogers*

When I was ten years old, my father arranged for cowboy legend Roy Rogers to teach me how to bowl. I'm not kidding. How my father managed to persuade Mr. Rogers to climb down from Trigger for an evening of gutter balls is beyond me. Although if you visit the Roy Rogers–Dale Evans Museum in Branson, Missouri, you will discover that the best exhibit is his collection of bowling trophies. An avid interest in strikes and spares, however, hardly explains my good fortune. Both my father and Mr. Rogers are no longer here to ask for the real reason. I do still wonder, though, why my father thought of Mr. Rogers and bowling in the same thought. I would like to think that my father believed that (1) somehow Mr. Rogers would make a better bowling instructor and (2) a ten-year-old boy might be more likely to follow the advice of one of his heroes.

Anyway, that's the sort of convoluted logic that led me to ask Bob Marks to help our program at Albuquerque Academy. I knew that he was better at coaching certain events than I, and I suspected that some students might be more likely to take his advice. Bob's background in professional theater prepared him to prepare students for acting careers. In short, his strengths shored up my weaknesses.

Over the years, I came to believe that Bob Marks may well have been the best high school speech coach in America. I do not say that lightly. Before I invited him to share his expertise with my team at Albuquerque Academy, I coached against him for more than a decade. When we finally started working together, I witnessed remarkable transformations in some of my students.

But the "Bob" Factor is not really about Bob. All teachers have weaknesses: unfamiliarity with certain parts of the curriculum, the inability to relate to certain personality types, not wanting to carefully correct papers. Even great teachers have their not-so-great moments. The key to overcoming these shortcomings is to find your "Bob." Someone you can bring into the classroom to do what you don't do so well. Sometimes a videotaped program can substitute for that person. Whatever it takes to help students maximize their potential, though, is what has to be done.

Not everyone can find a "Bob" comparable to mine. I would venture to say that no one can. So begin building a brain trust—a collection of people who have different, complementary skills to offer. My brain trust consisted of former students. Trained by me, they knew the philosophy of the program and the level of excellence expected. All teachers have former students. Call on them. They can make a difference for future students.

And there will be happy trails for everyone.

WHEN THEY GET IT

PUJA BHATIA

LOGAN HIGH SCHOOL

UCLA student

I remember it was my senior year and I was struggling with my oratory. It was about listening and how our society tunes out because everyone is just too busy. I thought it was an interesting topic, considering one of the fundamentals of speech and debate is the ability to listen. But for many reasons, my oratory lacked the energy that it really needed. I couldn't explain what that energy was, but I knew my recipe for an oratory was a few ingredients short.

Then Mr. Lindsey told me about this man, Mr. Marks, who I had never heard of. He was supposed to be an oratory wiz, and his ability to help students with their oratories was displayed by a history of national championships. At this point, I needed anything that could bring my oratory back to life. After I walked into the room for a practice session with Mr. Marks, I began to recite my speech. Two minutes into the speech, he stopped me and made me deliver the whole thing again. My voice had always carried in a room, especially because I was tall, but I didn't know how to use every corner of the room and every audience member to my advantage. He worked on my hand gestures—I never knew that hands should only go up at certain parts of an oratory. I always used my hand gestures when I thought appropriate, and I never thought there was a formula to the gestures. Mr. Marks helped me deliver my poorly written jokes through changing just my body language. For the first hour, it was a crash course on delivery, something I initially didn't think I needed after competing for four years. But that crash course was so important because those four years had made me too comfortable in the way I spoke so I never once had questioned my delivery as perhaps being part of the reason why the recipe was not working.

For that hour, we went through line after line and scripted the way I had to deliver it with hand, body, and face synchronized in their gestures. Then we began to work on the writing of the oratory. One thing I realized about Mr. Marks was that he was always thinking of how to put a twist to the most normal statement. While I gave my speech, he sporadically thought of jokes and puns that made my oratory more entertaining. It felt like the pieces were slowly coming together. He knew stories or references to stories that could better express the seriousness of my oratory in order to keep the audience captivated. He gave my oratory a more solid vehicle—a motif that runs throughout a speech in order to tie all of your points together. It felt like this man was an Internet search engine because his knowledge about some of the most random facts was amazing.

Mr. Marks also came with our team to Atlanta for an invitational tournament. At that tournament, he made sure to check what I was wearing during my oratory rounds. I had to wear dark-colored stockings, and I had to wear my hair up, because otherwise people would be distracted from my face and what I was saying. I never realized how much went into the event of oratory until meeting Mr. Marks.

Mr. Marks may be the best at what he does. Not only did he help me spice up the recipe of my oratory, but he also showed me how to change my delivery. Never would I have thought that after four years, one practice session with Mr. Marks would make me rethink the fundamental ways I spoke or presented myself in forensics. I am truly grateful for what he taught me.

READING ALLOWED

Randy

I do not like green eggs and ham. —*Dr. Seuss*

When Dr. Seuss died, an entire nation mourned. Appearing on the television program "Saturday Night Live," the Reverend Jesse Jackson read from Dr. Seuss's beloved story *Green Eggs and Ham*. It was a fitting tribute: millions of children had grown up in a world peopled by Hunches in Bunches and Brown Bar-ba-loots. For many students, their first experience with reading aloud may have been when one of their parents interpreted Dr. Seuss for them: "I do not like green eggs and ham. I do not like them, Sam-I-am."

I believe that many students miss out on the joy of reading because they stop hearing voices. As they grow older, they no longer allow themselves to imagine a unique speaking voice for each character in a book. They forget that Grandpa should sound different than Grandma. And they both should sound unlike little Cousin

Charlie. They forget that even the narrator of a story can have a personality that comes through in the telling of what happens.

If we fail to teach students how to interpret literature orally, then we are taking away much of the fun of reading. Furthermore, those students will be unable to make literature someday come alive as they read to their children. This unfortunate cycle endangers the future of reading.

There was a time when reading aloud played an important role in the cultural history of our country. Before radio and television, many families would read aloud in the evenings. Young children, spellbound by the great works of literature, would spend hours in shared adventure. Much as musicians give concerts today, oral interpreters in the early 1900s would go on tour. These tours brought entertainment and culture to even the most remote regions of our country.

The current popularity of slam poetry and of performance poetry offers some hope, though. Purists say that slam poetry is not performance poetry. Slam poetry is essentially poetry that is being performed and not a performance that includes poetry. I am not a purist. In my classroom, any activity that engages students in reading aloud is beneficial. To prepare for these activities, though, a student must learn to use his or her voice and body effectively. I would recommend that teachers read the "Oral Interpretation" chapter in the textbook *Glencoe Speech*. This chapter trains the reader in the skills necessary to be an effective interpreter.

When I taught oral interpretation as a graduate teaching assistant in college, three couples met in my classes and later were married. Many reasons could explain their coupling, but I think they came together in part because of the nature of oral interpretation. Students were required to read from works of literature that had special meaning for them. These weekly assignments—and the subsequent personal revelations—brought everyone in the class closer together. The students read what they loved. And those students who cared about the same things found each other.

PRACTICAL MATTERS

WORKS OF LITERATURE SPEAK

Works of literature speak to each other. When students are asked to connect multiple selections in a program of oral interpretation, they begin to understand the shared meanings and feelings of those works. This activity asks students to find two poems that are connected in some way. Tell the students to seek thematic unity.

Granger's Index to Poetry is an excellent reference tool for putting together this kind of oral interpretation program. The subject index will lead the reader to numerous poems on hundreds of topics. Entries in the subject index range from the Civil War to Christmas cards, from funerals to furniture. Students will find references to poems that may plant the seeds of curiosity, such as "Ode to a Pig While His Nose Was Being Bored," "Elegy for the Monastery Barn," and "Cupid the Ploughboy." In short, there's something for everyone.

Before the student reads two poems aloud, however, he or she should prepare an introduction that explains the "connection." What follows is an introduction I prepared to show students an example of what was expected of them. The works of literature in this program are conversing about the mysteries of mirrors.

If you look in a mirror and raise one hand, which hand are you really raising in your mirror image? Joyce Carol Oates poses this question in her poem "Love Letter, with Static Interference from Einstein's Brain." Perhaps Oates borrowed this mirror motif from a story about Lewis Carroll reported in the London *Times* on January 22, 1932.

According to this story, Carroll asked his cousin Alice Raikes in which hand she held an orange. Alice replied, "The right." So Carroll asked the young girl to stand before a mirror and tell him in which hand she now held the orange. And Alice replied, "The left."

For you see, in a mirror, all asymmetrical objects go the other way. So let us go the other way, through the looking glass—that is poetry. We begin our journey with Ishmael Reed's "beware do not read this poem."*

---

*Reed's poem is about an "ol woman, so vain she surrounded herself w/ many mirrors."

WHEN THEY GET IT

LANNA JOFFREY

ALBUQUERQUE ACADEMY

Writer, actress, teacher

To me, epiphanies are moments of clarity. When you suddenly notice your vision has sharpened; everything and everyone is a clear crisp image. You know that where you are at that moment is where you are supposed to be. I distinctly remember a moment of clarity in my seventh grade English class. We had the new teacher, Randy McCutcheon. He had asked us to answer the unanswerable questions of why the sky is blue and what is life.

I remember reading aloud how I thought life was like a walk along a tightrope. Every step deeply mattered, and one false move could throw off the balance, but most of the time you had a net and it was OK. Death was the day you slipped and the net wasn't there. I shyly looked up, ready for my peers to laugh. I had been laughed at before in Mr. Hannum's class from another writing assignment, but Randy didn't let anyone laugh. He looked at me in sincere awe and said he couldn't believe at my age I could answer the unanswerable. My fearful expression shifted into a wide smile and everything was clear and crisp. His sincerity and praise gave me permission to think I was capable and talented, that I had something worth sharing. He encouraged me with quotes and books by W. H. Auden, Ellen Goodman, Elie Wiesel, Lorrie Moore, John Updike, and Sally Hayton-Keeva.

Sally was especially important in my life. Randy gave me *Valiant Women in War and Exile*, a book of interviews sharing women's firsthand experiences of war throughout the twentieth century. I read the book in an awkward time of my life, at age sixteen, when

I questioned what my place was in the world. My parents and Randy said I could be anything I wanted to be, but was that true? There seemed to be so many professions almost completely dominated by men: politicians, directors, writers, police officers, playwrights, engineers, doctors—the list seemingly went on and on. My world of possibilities seemed small. The book expanded this world exponentially with each story I read: the words of women who defied these small notions. I really could be anything. If girls younger than me could survive such atrocities and still continue on, then high school was not such a daunting task. I was struck with another moment of clarity and was deeply inspired.

Many, many years past my sixteenth birthday, I contacted Sally, who immediately granted me the rights to adapt her book into a play. Three years and nine drafts later, I have come to *Valiant*, a docudrama using the exact word-for-word interviews of thirteen women. I recently went back to high school to perform this play, and in the audience was Randy, who watched one of his students continue to answer unanswerable questions.

Healthy Self-Expression

Tommie

It is the supreme art of the teacher to awaken joy
in creative expression and knowledge.

—*Albert Einstein*

One of the true pleasures I've discovered through speech is to be able to teach material to students and for them to allow their creativity to take over. When students enter as freshmen, they have no idea what they're doing. However, by their sophomore and junior years, they have been able to watch their teammates, and their creativity begins to develop. It is an amazing metamorphosis as you see shy kids turn into mature, outspoken individuals. And you watch as reluctant speakers become confident and determined orators.

It isn't until students videotape themselves giving practice speeches that they see how embarrassed, self-conscious, and unpolished they must appear to the audience. The nervous teen-agers on the television screen keep fidgeting with a sliver of fabric on their clothes while their bodies sway to an uneven rhythm. And though their eyes dart left and right, the pair are often riveted to the carpet as mumblings of semigrammatically correct sentences tumble out of their mouths. It isn't a pretty sight. But everyone faces the same problems.

Videotaped practices are a rite of passage for all beginning speech and debate students. The experience is both humbling and painful—flaws in one's own speaking style become obvious when one switches from performer to judge. But the implications of poor speaking skills run deeper than results in forensics com-petitions. The way a person speaks in public is intimately tied to one's self-image and self-confidence. Moreover, poor presentation skills act as formidable barriers to others taking you and your ideas seriously.

As a forensics coach, I have the responsibility to ensure that students learn to express themselves in a healthy, positive way. Albert Einstein was right to call it the "supreme art." I've found no greater joy than watching Eric Tam, a student who couldn't speak English when he came to America, develop into not only a great speaker but also an outstanding writer.

Eric Tam
Logan High School

When I saw my own tapes, I decided that my unsophisticated tongue and high school slang could be interpreted by the casual observer as immaturity or, worse, lacking of substantive ideas. High school students—like myself at that time—rarely possess confidence and polish in speech, partly because they are inexperienced in speaking to an audience. But the root cause can be traced to an unhealthy self-image. I remember presenting in front of class and using fillers like "umm" or looking down and scratching my head when advancing possibly incorrect arguments. Other times I spoke softly and guardedly when cold-called upon to answer questions in class because a weak and uncontroversial answer allowed me to hedge against being wrong. These unconscious cues are elements of unhealthy self-expression and reflected an undervaluation of the validity of my ideas and the respect they deserved.

Fortunately, my desire to improve and the many hours of practice yielded great results. My new ability to speak articulately and engagingly about any topic boosted my confidence, and today I am no longer shy about vigorously expressing my ideas. In addition to the success and opportunities these skills granted me in college and my career, I live a more fulfilling life because of the healthy self-image I developed through speech and debate. I did not enjoy the videotaped practices nor do I relish remembering the awkward teenager appearing on my tapes, but it was partly in that crucible that I was transformed.

As teachers, we hope that students will eventually learn that self-expression is about more than simple persuasion. Healthy self-expression requires trust and respect. Trust and respect are earned by what we do.

Action indeed is the sole medium of expression for ethics.

—*Jane Addams*

WHEN THEY GET IT

PARESH MAKAN

LOGAN HIGH SCHOOL

Santa Clara University School of Law student

As a law student and former editor in chief of Logan's newspaper, I'm all about facts. When I joined the forensics team in tenth grade, there were some facts about the team that were hard to ignore. We were a broad cross-section of students—there were the honors kids, the athletes, the overachievers, and what some would call the underachievers. We were from a public school in a middle-class community that didn't have a tradition of achievement in public speaking (at least not before Mr. Lindsey came along). By any measure, we weren't the typical forensics team. The odds were against us, and the team had more than its fair share of critics who reminded us of this fact. But for me, the most important fact was, and is, that we defied the odds every weekend. So I knew when I joined the team that I was part of something special, although the true value of the team in my life didn't become apparent until I got to law school.

As a second-year law student, I participated in the school's annual Honors Moot Court competition where, with a partner, I argued a case as if it were before the United States Supreme Court. My partner and I found ourselves in the final round of the competition facing a panel of judges that included two United States District Court judges, two Santa Clara County Superior Court judges, and Justice Raymond C. Fisher of the United States Ninth Circuit Court of Appeals. Justice Fisher was the most senior judge I'd ever seen, let alone argued before. We were all onstage in the recital hall; I had a microphone and a panel of five judges in front of me, a video camera trained on my face, and three hundred people sitting behind me, scrutinizing my every word and movement. In all my years on the forensics team, I never had been in a situation even remotely as imposing and intimidating as this one.

I was arguing for the petitioner on the first claim, which meant I had the honor of being the first to get up and speak. I did extemporaneous speaking in high school, and as such I was not accustomed to having a prepared text. I had spoken off the cuff in the previous rounds, but I didn't think it would be enough for the final round. So for the first time in the competition, I had actually prepared a text for my argument. I didn't make it more than two minutes into my argument when the barrage of questions by the judges began. For the next thirteen minutes, a nonstop flurry of questions came my way. There was no way of stopping to look at my text. The judges wanted answers, they wanted them now, and it just wasn't going to cut it if I said, "Give me just one minute to look at my text." I automatically fell back on the skills I had developed from doing debate and extemporaneous speaking in high school. I answered their questions and made my arguments without once looking down or pausing. My fifteen minutes, which seemed more like fifty, finally ended, and I sat down literally exhausted. My partner and I ended up winning the competition, and I also won Best Oral Advocate for the two preliminary rounds.

You hear a lot about epiphanies—those singular moments of clarity when by some divine intervention, it all makes sense. I'd never experienced such a moment until I drove home that night. I realized that being a lawyer takes more than just going to law school and passing the bar exam. More than anything, the practice of law is about being an *advocate* for our clients. It is about arguing the client's case, convincing others we're right, and at the same time earning the trust, respect, and confidence of both the court and client. One can go to school and learn the law, but the actual advocacy can only be learned through experience—experience I was lucky enough to have gained from the forensics team. I have always wanted to be a lawyer, and I probably could have come to law school and learned the law even if I hadn't been on the forensics team. However, I definitely could not have become an advocate without forensics.

PRACTICAL MATTERS

MOCK ENCOMIUMS AND OTHER PROPOSALS

Jonathan Swift and Mark Twain were masters of the mock encomium, a form of satire in which pretended praise is actually blame. The mock encomium tantalizes students. They can become extremely passionate when asked to argue badly for the side they oppose. Swift's "A Modest Proposal" inspires them to write their own proposals. Just remind them that in 1729, Swift, in response to the Irish economic crisis, argued that Ireland should start exporting their children—not only as servants but as the main ingredient in cooking recipes.

Students also find Mark Twain's skill as a satirist inspiring. His "War Prayer," a mock encomium treatment of the Spanish-American War, appears to ask God to help our soldiers "tear their soldiers to bloody shreds." Students soon catch on to Twain's real intention.

I assign students to write their own mock encomiums. One student, for example, advocated having all women drafted into the military. She used, in part, the argument that then women wouldn't have so much trouble deciding what to wear. I made her research what a woman in the army would really wear (so she could include specific details about their uniforms). The only way this assignment works is if the students understand that they have to have actual content. Otherwise, the students will merely rant and rave.

Other forms of satire encourage creativity as well. Students find composing a parody a challenging exercise. Students need to understand that the parody exaggerates certain characteristics of another work of art, but that the original work is still recognizable. Borrow a Weird Al Yankovic CD for some fun examples.

I found it helpful to show them some parodies of literature and historical documents. Following is my parody of the Gettysburg Address from the book *Get Off My Brain*.

The I-Get-So-Bored Address
(with apologies to one of our tallest presidents)

Nobody kept score and many cheers ago, our poor teachers brought forth the concept, conceived in mediocrity, that all students are created equal and therefore need only be "equally creative."

Now we are engaged in a back-to-basics bedlam. We have made our bedlam, but it is the students who must lie in it. Therefore, it is altogether fitting and proper that we should stop lying.

But in a larger sense, we can no longer demonstrate, we can no longer educate, we can no longer create in the classroom. The brave minds, dead and dying, who struggled there, may never create, but they can add and subtract. True, the world will little note nor long remember what we say here, but generations of students will be forced to memorize it verbatim and pass a true-false test.

And so it is rather for us the thinking to abhor the dead minds and spreading behinds with our last full measure of revulsion; that we here highly resolve that there must be a new birth of free thinking, and that the creativity of the students, by the students and for the students, shall not perish from education.

GLOSSOPHOBIA

Randy

You're listening to KRFS, 1600 on your radio dial.
Broadcasting live from Superior.

—*DJ Randy McCutcheon*

W hen you reach a certain age in a small town, you have
to get a job. Otherwise, the neighbors start to talk. Much
blabbing about bums over the backyard fence, if you catch my
drift. For me, two options availed themselves. Stuffing grocery
bags at a local supermarket or announcing on weekends at the
town's 500 watt radio station. Well, public speaking terrified me
(despite my semisuccessful stint as a high school debater), but
actual work was out of the question. How hard could it be to say,
"It's 9:47 on a Saturday morning. That was Elton John with 'Your
Song,' and here are the Beatles." Little did I know.

On this particular AM station, we read the news twice an hour. Seconds before the newsbreak, we would "rip and read" wire service reports from a machine provided by the Associated Press. Sounds easy, eh? Unfortunately, the copy sometimes looked like it was encoded by the CIA:

Washington, D.C.—President Johnson held a press conference today in the nation's capital. He said that he was deeply concerned about kefftpqry ogmlad ifjswwom. . . .

And I would ad-lib, ". . . that he was deeply concerned about the future of our country," or something equally generic. It was at these moments I discovered the true meaning of *glossophobia*. Real fear will make you gloss over anything.

I remember the first early morning farm report I read. I pronounced *ewes* as if the word rhymed with *kiwis*. No listener called in to correct me. Perhaps they thought the error was a welcome attempt at ovine joviality, or, more likely, we had no listeners. Perhaps my biggest blooper occurred while introducing our polka show one Sunday morning. I was supposed to say, "You're listening to KRFS in Superior, Nebraska. It's 11:30 and time now for the 'Happy Time Polka Party.'" My mind in a romantic haze, however, had wandered to the night before and to some serious smooching with my high school sweetheart. I said, "You're listening to KRFS in Superior, Nebraska. It's 11:30 and time now for the 'Happy Time Parkin' Polky.'"

Teachers know that the adolescent mind does a lot of wandering. And the fear of suddenly revealing something he doesn't want the whole world to know can be numbing to a teenage boy. Or girl. Adolescent angst, too, often intensifies the fear of opening one's mouth in public. Whatever the causes, the fear of public speaking can be debilitating to some students.

AMABELLE CAMINS
LOGAN HIGH SCHOOL

On the first day of the Forensics Summer Academy, I remember watching Charles Kuo and David Huang, the first members of Logan's forensics team, giving impromptu speeches. I was amazed at how they were able to fill five minutes with information—logical information at that! Then I became terrified that I was being asked by one of the assistant coaches to do the same thing! I'm thinking, "How can you expect me to follow experienced, seasoned orators?"

Needless to say, my performance was horrible. The three minutes of prep time felt like three seconds, and my mind was in a jumble. I stood in the middle of the room with my mind blank after about twenty seconds of speaking. I looked into expectant, waiting faces around the room and embarrassment washed over me. Thank goodness, my instructor was very kind and let me sit down after a few seconds, and we went on to the next speaker.

After the class, as students were preparing to go home, I approached Mr. Lindsey, to inform him that I had decided that forensics was not right for me. I knew when to accept my limitations and wanted to be up front that I would not return to class the next day. I expected Mr. Lindsey to respect my decision and wish me well.

"Mr. Lindsey," I began, "I don't think this is the right thing for me to do this summer."

Mr. Lindsey leaned back behind his desk and toyed with a pair of scissors. "Why not?" he asked. I started to tell him how my mind just did not work that fast and that I was not exposed to information that would be useful in any speeches. "This is the first day," Mr. Lindsey countered. "Just come back tomorrow and we'll see what happens." He then turned to address another student, giving me no chance to argue back.

I could not believe that this teacher was dismissing my fears and brushing aside my absolute terror of public speaking! "We'll see what happens!"—I don't think so!

I think I came back the next day if only to prove Mr. Lindsey wrong—that what would happen that day would be exactly what happened on that first day. I thought I would bomb each speech. What I didn't count on was that everybody else, aside from Charles and David, would do so, too. I would form a bond with my "miserable" classmates, and together we would forge ahead.

Of course, not all students will sign up for their school's speech team. Parents and teachers must take responsibility for those students. No student should leave high school without overcoming the fear of public speaking. Furthermore, each student should learn how to present ideas in a clear and meaningful way. To reach this goal, teachers need to design numerous lesson plans that require oral presentations. Meaningful feedback is a must.

A first step is to help students understand that the fear of public speaking is normal. If all the world's a stage, most of us players suffer from stage fright. Newsman Charles Osgood had an interesting theory on stage fright. Osgood said, "Have you ever been driving at night and come upon a deer frozen in the beam of your headlights? Here's my theory. The deer thinks the lights are spotlights, and what has it paralyzed is stage fright. It imagines the worst. It has to give a speech."

Let students know that the symptoms of nervousness are common among speakers of all ages. An upset stomach, a flushed face, dizziness, a fast heartbeat, shortness of breath, excessive breath, and wobbly legs—these can undermine anyone's confidence.

But why? Why do we get these symptoms? The first reason is that our bodies are flooded with energy. The body prepares for what it perceives to be an emergency situation. The second reason, though, is that we don't want to be evaluated or judged. Sometimes we don't think our ideas are worth listening to. Or we don't believe we can articulate our ideas effectively. Ultimately, we fear that people might not like us.

 JENNIFER CHANG KUO
LOGAN HIGH SCHOOL

Today, I feel like a confident, happy, and successful woman—and an articulate one. But I can't say the same of myself when I started high school. I was painfully shy—so shy, I even abhorred speaking to store clerks or waitresses. I didn't want to speak in public and definitely didn't like it. My only reason for joining the forensics team was because my brother had joined the year before, and I could see the benefits it would bring to me.

My very first speech for the forensics team was meant to be five minutes long—an impromptu, in front of a class of less than fifteen people. It doesn't sound intimidating. It shouldn't be frightening. But it was. I remember standing there for what seemed like an eternity, with a thousand abbreviated thoughts swirling through my mind, unable to form words. I knew my knees were shaking, and my voice was quivering—I was unable to make eye contact with anyone. My very first speech was an unmitigated disaster. In war, it would have been called a rout.

I was never one of the best speakers on the team. But over time, after hours and hours of work, long weekends, and many sweaty palms, I achieved an award of Outstanding Distinction from the National Forensic League. I must admit it was more from sheer stubbornness, time, and hard work rather than from talent. I knew which members of the team had talent—they were amazing. But for me, it was enough to get by. Today, my knees will still shake and my heart will still pound when I speak in public, but I can now project an image of calm and confidence. I have even been complimented on my public speaking.

In my first book, *Get Off My Brain*, I offered specific strategies for overcoming the fear of public speaking. After dismissing such ideas as the "Brady Bunch" approach of imagining the audience in their underwear or the often tried methods of staring at the foreheads or over the heads of audience members, I explain that there are two things the average person can do. The first is to make an *instant joke*. In other words, the split-second you are aware of your anxiety, you should say a one-liner (to yourself) and then quickly refocus your attention on the subject of your speech. Consider these examples:

- You feel drops of sweat pouring from your armpits and staining your shirt. You immediately say to yourself, in a jocular manner, "Great, I won't need to take a bath this week," and in an instant, you return your attention to the content of your presentation.
- You are certain that your heart is pounding so loudly that people in the back row are quaking from the vibrations. Using the same basic process as before, you say, "Hooray, maybe someone will finally ask me to dance."

The second thing for nervous speakers to try is *grinning*. For most people, smiling confidently and being nervous are incompatible physiological responses. With the exception of those few who giggle and turn silly during times of anxiety, smiling when confronting the symptoms of fear is immediately calming. The trick is to force yourself to smile the instant that you recognize the symptoms.

In a way, my two suggested "cures" for glossophobia are related. They are attempts to help students relax by smiling no matter what. Not a bad idea when you think about it.

WHEN THEY GET IT

DAWN CHARISSE MICHAEL, M.D.

LOGAN HIGH SCHOOL

Physician

I vividly remember my very first time stepping in front of the classroom to say my speech. Mr. Lindsey sat at the center of the room with a stern look, but also with a look of support and confidence. His expectations were made known by his disposition in itself. Mr. Lindsey did not settle for anything less than superb work and performance, so I knew that I had to snap out of my fear and perform! The first few seconds, I was so nervous, I almost forgot my speech. But I quickly imagined that I was the only one in the room and began my speech for fear of letting him down. At the time, I was performing my speech for him and the class, but really, I was learning so much more. I was learning how to overcome personal fears and obstacles, be determined, and persevere when things get tough.

Week after week, speech after speech, I became more and more confident, and these lessons became more ingrained into my personal mottoes. It was Mr. Lindsey's tough love that pushed me and all of my classmates to reach our peak and nothing short of that. When you thought you had done a great job, the best you could do, Mr. Lindsey would say, "Is that all you have? You could do better than that. Humph." And he was always right, because the next week, the next speech, we did do better, every single time.

The speaking skills that I gained in forensics aided me well throughout my college years at the University of Michigan. The clever debate skills I had acquired afforded me a position as a resident director in my senior year of college, a job that is historically offered only to graduate students. I finally realized how much my forensics experience with Mr. Lindsey was vital to my success once I began the tedious process of applying to medical school. I was admitted to all but one of the medical schools that I interviewed at over the entire country, not by merit alone but by the way that I verbally presented myself. After matriculating into medical school, I was a leader in national student groups, in community outreach, in academic groups, and in rotations in the hospital with senior residents and attendings because of my ability to communicate effectively, intelligently, and with a strong presence. Speaking with a presence is what Mr. Lindsey taught.

ASK AN EXPERT

Randy

Throughout my formal education I spent many,
many hours in public and school libraries.
Libraries became courts of last resort, as it were.
The current definitive answer to almost any
question can be found within the four walls of
most libraries.

—*Arthur Ashe*

Arthur Ashe's message to young men who thought they would someday be professional athletes was to spend more hours in the library. Ashe knew that the chances for becoming a professional athlete were slim. Other opportunities awaited those who were "not great but busy." But what should students be busy about?

One of the most important lessons for students to learn is to ask an expert. Experts provide the focus and direction necessary to launch any project. If a student is researching a paper on the changing economy in China, for example, should cyberspace be the place to start? Hardly. A history professor from a nearby college can recommend the specific books and articles to look for in the library. Professors dedicate their lives to being knowledgeable about their fields. And if the Chinese economy is not this professor's area of expertise, he or she can refer the student to a colleague. Most high school students are not aware that college professors have office hours each week. A phone call to the department office for those office hours is the first step. The student can always rely on dumb luck: just ask for any professor who is around at the moment.

The story I share with students to teach the "Ask an Expert" lesson involves a former student who attended the University of Kansas. In one of her journalism classes, the students were assigned to write an obituary for Wilbur Mills. The task was made a bit more challenging because Mr. Mills was still alive at the time. For those of you who don't remember the scandal, Mills, a member of the House of Representatives from Arkansas, was caught on film cavorting in the Tidal Basin with stripper Fanne Fox, the "Argentine Firecracker." Back in the 1970s, such carrying on could have dire consequences for a politician.

In our phone conversation, my student asked me what she should include in the obituary. After all, if she relied on the newspapers and popular periodicals in her college library, then most of the information would be about that scandal. Is it fair, she asked, to summarize a man's entire life in such a limited way?

My advice to her, I tell the students, was to call an expert. The expert in this case could be found in Mills's home state of Arkansas. I suggested that she call the *Arkansas Democrat-Gazette* in Little Rock. I told her to speak to any editor who would talk to her. All major newspapers have files on the leading citizens of their states. When the time comes, these newspapers have to be prepared to write meaningful obituaries, which would include a recounting of every significant contribution made by that particular citizen.

The second suggestion was to ask the editor from the *Arkansas Democrat-Gazette* how to contact Mills. It turns out that Mills was working at a law firm in Washington, D.C. The student called him at his office and was able to ask him how he wanted to be remembered by historians.

My final suggestion was simply to add footnotes to the obituary that documented the two phone conversations. The student aced the assignment. But what if she had relied on the popular periodicals of the day (or a Google search today)?

One of my students, Rani Waterman, was so inspired by the Wilbur Mills obituary saga that she made her own phone call. The world, she found out, was waiting for her to ask.

"WE COLLABORATE. I'M AN EXPERT, BUT NOT AN AUTHORITY, AND DR. GELPIS IS AN AUTHORITY, BUT NOT AN EXPERT."

When They Get It

Rani Waterman

Albuquerque Academy

Northwestern University graduate, actress

It was the Wimbledon of high school speech, the final round of original oratory at the Barkley Forum. After many rounds of verbal back-and-forth over the course of two days, the field had finally been narrowed down to six: myself and five others. As it was my senior year in high school, this was my last year to make my oral mark on speech history, my last chance to be a champion. I was sweating. I took a deep breath and scanned the audience—all two hundred attentive listeners waiting to hear what I thought about the world. I prayed silently that no one could see my knees shaking.

In the split second before beginning my speech, I thought back to how I got to this point: Charles Kuralt's book *On the Road with Charles Kuralt*. My speech coach, Randy, had brought it to me at the beginning of the year, telling me my oratory was in it somewhere. After spending fifteen years as the host of CBS's hit TV show "On the Road," Kuralt had passed away the previous July. In his time spent on the road, Kuralt interviewed hundreds of everyday people living in nowhere towns. Walter Cronkite said of Kuralt's reports, "[They] reminded people that all [was] not lost, that life has something of value for each one of us."

One of Kuralt's interviews was with a man named Eddie Lovett. An unlettered son of a sharecropper, Mr. Lovett turned himself into a formidable scholar. Mr. Lovett had a library: a lifetime accumulation of thousands of books, which he read day and night. When Kuralt dubiously asked what all his reading had done for him, Lovett replied, "I think it's doing me—particularly my children—a lot of good because to tell the truth, I'm really living for my children. I want to set a good example for them. I have to set the example."

When I read Mr. Lovett's story, I was entranced. Mr. Lovett had taken the road less traveled; he created a library, a lasting legacy for his children. Here was my oratory. The only problem was that I wanted to know more. I wondered how Mr. Lovett had received the news of Kuralt's death. I wanted to know how this interview had changed him, if at all. I wanted to know where his library was now. So, like any diligent student, I posed my questions to my coach, Randy. He said simply, "Call him up. Ask him." Huh. Hadn't thought of that one.

So, I went home that night, called information for Alabama, and within minutes was connected to Eddie Lovett. It didn't seem possible that a person I had read about in an obscure not-even-bestseller book was now on the other end of the telephone line. I explained my purpose for calling him, and he seemed astounded that I would be interested in writing a speech about him. Our conversation was brief (Mr. Lovett was not much of a talker), but he told me something I will never forget. When I questioned him about his meeting with Charles Kuralt, Mr. Lovett responded, "In a sense, he introduced me to the world."

And in a sense, Mr. Lovett had introduced me to a new part of the world. His world. With one phone call I finally did what AT&T had been telling me for years. I reached out into the ether and touched someone.

With that thought, I snapped back to my final round at Barkley. I smiled and relaxed, remembering what Eddie Lovett had taught me. The beauty of what I was doing there was the fact that for ten minutes, two hundred people were going to be listening to me, to my stories, to my thoughts. And perhaps it would affect them. I realized then that I was introducing all of *them* to a new world. My world.

Practical Matters

Forrester for the Trees

When it comes to changing instructional strategies, some English teachers are slower than Godot. If a student writer struggles, it's time to search for different answers. Sometimes, if you're fortunate, serendipity intervenes. The film *Finding Forrester* finally reached the top of my Netflix queue. The story follows the friendship of Jamal, a young black high school student, and William Forrester, who once wrote a Pulitzer Prize–winning novel. Although the plot is somewhat contrived, it's a wonderful film. For our purposes here, let me share one of Forrester's instructional strategies. An aspiring writer, Jamal struggles until Forrester gives him some of his own prose to jump-start the process. The idea was for Jamal to begin typing the first paragraph of Forrester's prose and then make it his own.

The success of this approach (at least in this feel-good film) reminded me of a strategy I employ in the teaching of writing. I ask students to use a work of literature, art, or music to organize an essay. This excerpt from Lanna Joffrey's persuasive essay should clarify what I mean.

"White. A blank page or canvas. The challenge: bring order to the whole. Through design, composition, balance, light, and harmony . . . So many possibilities." In these opening lines to the play *Sunday in the Park with George*, the character Georges Seurat envisioned an opening curtain rising, exposing an expanse of white, an expanse suggesting untouched life, a blank canvas. And through design, composition, balance, and light, the painting would achieve harmony and become complete. And the images on that canvas would come alive and so would that untouched life. Like the artist Seurat, each of us chooses the brushstrokes that become a life. Unfortunately, as we are making choices, too many of us let other people control what goes on our canvases. We let others paint our lives away by allowing them to choose for us.

In this essay, Lanna selected the play *Sunday in the Park with George* to create a framework for her thoughts. The parallels between a painting and a life gave direction to her argument that each of us should take control of what goes on our canvases.

Some other examples that link subject matter to artistic works include an essay on how fear adversely affects us throughout our lives (Shakespeare's "Seven Ages of Man"); an essay on the need for passion, humor, and spirituality in our lives (Beethoven's "Ode to Joy"); and an essay on the lack of uncommon sense in our society (a *Calvin and Hobbes* cartoon).

To read numerous "completed" examples of this strategy, check out the books *Great Student Speeches* and *Glencoe Speech* (both available from Glencoe/McGraw-Hill).

"Let's go." "Yes, let's go." (They do not move.)
—*Samuel Beckett,* Waiting for Godot

THE ART OF PERSUASION

Randy

I'm not sure what his points are, but without
knowing what his points are, I'd say he has some
good points.

—John McEnroe on the comments of another player

Put another nickel in the slot. The Hotel Leslie, early Saturday mornings, 1963—before the Beatles invaded Nebraska.
Another silver ball pops in the lane. Pull the plunger—the game
is on. The ball careens perilously: ding, ding, ding; bumpers rico-
chet: ding, ding, ding. Fippers frozen: pshaw—not enough points
for a free game. Oh, no—pockets emptier than promises. . . .

"Son, you know that playing pinball is the smartest thing you
could be doing. A lot of young men make a fine living doing
just what you're doing right now. Throwing away money on these

games is a great idea. Most successful men would agree with that."

The insurance agent, who had an office in the hotel lobby right next to my electronic light and sound show, had chosen this inopportune moment to interrupt my reverie. I wasn't exactly sure what he meant, but I knew he had a good point.

"Say, mister, could you loan me a nickel until next Saturday?"

In graduate school, I can remember eager Ph.D. candidates asserting that all communication is persuasion. Of course, those discussions were long after my days of pinball wizardry and long before John McEnroe held a microphone. Whether or not you think McEnroe was ever serious, we need to teach students the art of persuasion.

When presenting persuasion strategies, most teachers introduce the students to Aristotle's three forms of proof: ethos, pathos, and logos.

- *Ethos* (or ethical proof) refers to the speaker's personal appeal—her credibility.
- *Pathos* (or emotional proof) aims straight for the heart, appealing to a person's feelings of love, anger, fear, compassion, and so on.
- *Logos* (or logical proof) is an appeal to a person's analytic side, offering solid reasoning and valid evidence.

True, these three concepts are important for students to understand and employ. What we don't spend enough time teaching, though, is integrity. We touch on the need for integrity as we explain ethos, but somehow the message isn't getting through. Students are exposed every day to people without integrity who seemingly go unpunished. Certainly, cheating, for example, is increasing among students. At this writing, one study (from the Center for Academic Integrity) revealed that more than 75 percent of American college students admitted cheating on tests or written assignments. Alarmingly, the percentage of students "actually *caught* cheating is a mere 5 percent."

What does this widespread cheating have to do with the art of persuasion, you may well ask. Quintilian, the Roman rhetoric teacher speaking centuries ago, argued, "The perfect orator is a good man speaking well." Although Quintilian would have said a "good person" today, the truth in his observation is inescapable. A good person does not cheat. Not on tests. Not in life. It is not the gift of gab, carefully rehearsed gestures, emotional appeals, nor a booming voice that should bring you success. Instead, the winning combination in persuasive communication should be an honest, positive message, hard work, and caring for your audience—in short, being a good person speaking well.

Integrity is not a 90 percent thing, not a 95 percent thing; either you have it or you don't.

—*Peter Scotese, retired CEO of Spring Industries*

 JERRI KAY-PHILLIPS
LOGAN HIGH SCHOOL

One of the toughest challenges I have faced not only in high school but also in life is trying to express myself to people who are generally close-minded. The close-mindedness of U.S. society seems magnified in high school; everyone is trying to find their niche and trying to be the cool kid. In such a chaotic mix of peer pressure, exclusion, and teen angst, it is very difficult to express ideas that do not always conform to the normal. A prime example happened when I was talking to a friend I had known for seven years. One day the topic of gay marriage came up, something that had appeared repeatedly in the news. My friend was opposed to gay marriage while I was for it. We argued ceaselessly, unable to even agree to disagree. We eventually left the argument feeling bitter and frustrated because we had not been able to get our point across.

But in Mr. Lindsey's class, even when topics of deep division and personal rancor come up in discussion, this sort of antagonism never happens. While the class rarely agrees and while the debates and arguments can become loud and boisterous, they never breed any sort of antagonism or moral contempt. This is because Mr. Lindsey has a very simple philosophy that all people ought to adhere to: "if it doesn't bother me, why should I care?" This life message has certainly made the class more open. The forensics class is the only class I have ever been in in which I never felt afraid to talk about anything. Students who have different lifestyles from the norm also are able to voice their personal stories and are not judged.

It would seem to me that this pluralism in the classroom is very much dependent on the teacher, because the teacher is the one who sets class policy and acts as a mentor, despite limits, to the students. Even when arguments are taken to a more personal level, the respect Mr. Lindsey commands because of his accepting way means that students will eventually quiet down. I think that one of the most important aspects of my four-year journey in forensics was learning that I should never be afraid to say what is on my mind and should always listen to what others have to say. This was rarely expressed to me in any of my other classes or indeed by any person before Mr. Lindsey showed me that arguments could be constructive rather than adversarial.

Character is the most effective means of persuasion.

—*Aristotle*

WHEN THEY GET IT

ARTHUR CHU

ALBUQUERQUE ACADEMY

Financial analyst

Most of the time, it is possible to muddle through days, weeks, and years without much understanding of what is going on around you (this is unfortunate but true). On the other hand, some of the most important and memorable moments in life are those when you realize what you are actually doing.

After half a year of attending various rounds of Lincoln-Douglas debate, I had a vague feeling for the form of the activity: there was apparently a prescribed formula that involved presenting values and value criteria, throwing in a marginally relevant quote from *A Theory of Justice*, using the word *ought* as often as possible, and trying not to talk too fast (this was reserved for the policy-debate types). I knew, though, that I wasn't really doing it correctly; it was hard to understand why anyone would believe what I was saying. More to the point, it wasn't easy to find examples of anyone who could seem to do it correctly (no obvious disrespect meant to my former colleagues). Certainly, there were more experienced debaters locally who stumbled less when they spoke and had a better mastery of the formula, but their style was flat and probably not persuasive to anyone who did not have explicit knowledge of what an L-D round was supposed to be—the speech equivalent of music without feeling or sports without athletic grace. There had to be more to this activity.

Despite my overall lack of competence, I was somehow conferred the privilege of attending my first national tournament (which, in fact, was the first national tournament of that year) at the beginning of the following season. Needless to say, I didn't do very well. My main accomplishment was showing up to view the final round, which actually turned out to be a meaningful accomplishment. The finalists were fluid and natural as they spoke. They told jokes, and they sweated significantly less than I did in the humid 80° weather. But these two were more than polished versions of the local competition I had seen previously: it was the first time that I had seen a debate where the participants would actually be persuasive to a more general audience, as opposed to only those obsessed with the form of the high school Lincoln-Douglas activity. Adherence to the rules of the debate was loose. Not every point was rebutted, nor were tortured, pseudophilosophical arguments (which few high school students, and even fewer adults, would understand) used for their own sake. Simple but accurate analogies made the point more clearly, and the finalists knew how to boil down the debate to just a few key arguments. I don't recall anyone screaming "ought" at the top of his lungs. The purpose of the debate was to communicate and persuade, and although everyone in the room knew this, few had actually internalized it. That round hit me over the head; I realized what I was doing.

FALLING IN LOVE WITH BOOKS

Randy

Outside of a dog, a book is a man's best friend.
Inside of a dog, it's too dark to read.

—Groucho Marx

In *The Literary Life and Other Curiosities,* author Robert Hendrickson introduces us to Joseph Feldman, a New York attorney. Although Feldman never bothered to get a library card, he managed to accumulate more than fifteen thousand "overdue" books from the New York Public Library. These books were accidentally discovered by firefighters during a routine inspection that followed a fire on the floor below Feldman's apartment. When questioned about why he had hoarded thousands of books, Feldman replied, "I love to read."

Wouldn't it be wonderful if students shared Feldman's passion (without the criminal tendencies) for books? Sadly, the lives of many students are more wonder-empty than wonder-full. It's not just the failure to read, though. The challenge for teachers is made more difficult because so many students question the value of what they are learning. These students echo Homer Simpson's doubts. Homer observes, "Every time I learn something new, it pushes some old stuff out of my brain. Remember when I took that home winemaking course, and I forgot how to drive?"

We may chuckle at Homer's rather disturbing naivete, but some students buy into the idea that they are wasting their time in school. They think they are wasting their time when they read books. Learning has little allure for them. Loving books? Not likely.

Kylene Beers, a professor of reading at the University of Houston, says, "About 100 percent of first-graders walk in on the first day and are interested in this thing called reading. Eighty percent of graduating seniors tell us they will never voluntarily pick up a book again."

When I discussed this phenomenon with a group of teachers in Virginia, they informed me that based on their experience the 80 percent figure was low. All teachers and parents should be shocked by this revelation. The consequence of not reading is a self-perpetuating cycle. Students who do not read do not develop their reading skills. Frustrated by their inability to learn, these students read less and less.

Illiteracy, therefore, is no longer the crisis. Aliteracy is far more alarming. Students can read. They choose not to. In the *Washington Post* article "The No-Book: Skim It and Weep," *aliteracy* is described as "an invisible liquid, seeping through our culture, nigh on impossible to pinpoint or defend against."

The pervasiveness of aliteracy may be surprising to some. After all, in one survey, 82 percent of Americans said they wanted to write a book. Pat Schroeder, president of the Association of American Publishers, commented, "Now if we can get 82 percent of Americans to read a book, we'd be in great shape."

 ROBERT HAWKINS
LOGAN HIGH SCHOOL

In the canon of my life, Mr. Lindsey's influence has been profound. George C. Wolfe, Arthur Miller, and even Eric Bogosian fell into my lap, when other courses those years were grounded in more traditional works. It was this deviation that allowed me to connect to all literature and, inevitably, to fall into words.

I am now and forever challenging all things I deem unfulfilling and pedestrian. Like a young John Keats, I struggle with what legacy I can create, one that will withstand the test of time despite the ever-looming realities of life. Life will teach me what "is." But, like any larger-than-life figure, Mr. Lindsey always imbued in me the possibility of passion and hope.

Perhaps the only viable way to "shape up" is to find those teachers who are succeeding at getting students to fall in love with books. I offer—for your consideration—the strategies employed by two of my childhood teachers. Their methods are not *the* solution. Clearly, you can reach children in different ways. But they do serve as examples of teachers who cared enough to try.

Miss Moffat, my first grade teacher, didn't mess around with hoping that her young charges would be eager to learn. The skits we performed each day created their own kind of eagerness. Burned in my memory is the image of Miss Moffat, surprisingly skilled at fisticuffs, flattening a first grade boy with a sly left hook. These skits were not for the fainthearted. At the end of each school day, Miss Moffat would stand at the classroom door. Handing each of us a lemon drop as we left, she would say that she wanted to make sure we would come back the next day.

But what I remember most about that year is her devotion to reading. Along one wall of our classroom loomed an imposing bookshelf—divided into sections, she explained, so that we could test ourselves. Each section had a dozen or so books at a specific reading level. Miss Moffat said we should start with the books at the first grade reading level and then progress to the second grade and so on. The idea was to see how far we could get. After a few months, I finished the books meant for fifth graders. Think what you want, but I know that Miss Moffat's belief in me made the difference.

Speaking of fifth grade, my teacher that year sponsored a contest that offered to the winner, she said, a Big Prize. The rules: for one semester, you were to read as many books as possible and, for each book, submit a written summary of what you learned. The student who read the most books would win the Big Prize. It was a contest right out of a Jean Shepherd story. Each day, I read another book. Every single day. Now I admit that many of the books were chosen because they contained the fewest number of pages. At the end of the semester, I edged out a seriously studious girl who probably deserved to win. My Big Prize: a book. I blurted out,

"Where's the Samsonite luggage, the Chevy convertible?" Not really. But I was disappointed. Much of my youth was spent chewing on the ol' irony sandwich. But this teacher meant well when she gave me my first dictionary. And she gave me a far greater gift: the habit of reading something every day.

Times have changed, though. How can we make reading more engaging to students today? Let's use the teaching of poetry as an example. Many high school students are turned off to poetry because we insist on what I call the albatross approach. Like the sailor in the Coleridge poem, we insist on killing something good as we give students the bird. Instead, we should begin our study of poetry with poems that just might tickle a student's fancy. Lawrence Ferlinghetti's "The World Is a Beautiful Place," Sharon Olds's "Topography," Leonard Cohen's "The Music Crept by Us," and E. E. Cummings's "nobody loses all the time" come to mind for me. The students find themselves attracted to the irreverence. The cleverness. In the twinkling of a sigh, no students are saying, "I hate poetry." And the door to possibility opens. Enter: Shakespeare, no longer pursued by a hard to bear.

WHEN THEY GET IT

SARAH SHUN-LIEN BYNUM

MILTON ACADEMY

2004 finalist for a National Book Award in Fiction (for Madeleine Is Sleeping*); her short story "Accomplice" was selected for* The Best American Short Stories 2004

I knew even then. On the final exam that year, students were asked to write a single essay. I encouraged Sarah to ignore my topic and create her own. I assured her that the topic she created would be far more interesting than mine. What follows are some of her thoughts about learning to love new writers.

What made that year so important to me: you gave me the freedom to bring all the outrageous, antisocial, countercultural stuff I loved into the classroom and instead of dismissing it or being offended by it, you embraced it as part of a much broader literary tradition and then, in turn, you taught Shakespeare and Dickinson and Eliot with the same urgency and passion with which I loved Jim Carroll and Lester Bangs—so that I learned to love all these writers in the same breath.

Curiously enough, my love for Eliot has far outlasted my affection for Kerouac or Bangs or Bukowski, but I still have an old fondness for them. I will *always* remember how you taught "Prufrock"—and in fact, I borrowed a line (the patient etherized on the table) for one of the last sections of my book. Anyhow, this was a long tangent—what I really wanted to say was, at the end of first semester, I performed a monologue by Edie Sedgwick, the Warhol It Girl and drug addict, with whom I was quite obsessed at the time. And in a miracle of things coming full circle, I have recently met and become friends with Jean Stein, the author of the definitive Edie biography that inspired my dramatic monologue for your class! Which is only to say, sophomore year English is still very much with me—it has cast a long and lovely shadow over the subsequent seventeen years.

PEOPLE FEEL YOU

Tommie

People feel you more than they hear you.

—*Al Sharpton*

I t has been said that when you meet someone face to face, more than 90 percent of how you are judged is based on nonverbal data: your appearance and your body language. Only 7 percent is influenced by words that you speak. People are definitely judged by first impressions. It doesn't matter whether it's your tone over the phone or your personal appearance. Clearly, as Al Sharpton so aptly put it, people feel you more than they hear you. My student Paul competed in Lincoln-Douglas debate and extemporaneous speaking in high school. In his spare time now, he helps coach the team and is truly a role model for my younger students. He explains his philosophy.

Paul Baldo

Logan High School

The usage of words and combinations of words—sentences—is an extremely important form of communication. However, actions *still* speak louder than words. For example, I can tell a person "I love you," but if I do not express that love through actions—hugging, holding hands, kissing—the claim of love is empty. Actions substantiate words and words are manifested and reinforced by actions. Consequently, the "authenticating-words" role that actions play makes actions more important than words.

Body language is one of the strongest forms of communication because it is universally understood. Generally, a head nod is universally accepted as the act of giving consent. Moreover, there are many actions that are expressed and felt without requiring the help of words. We can make someone uncomfortable or feel ignored simply by not facing him or her while he or she is speaking to us. In general, words require actions for authentication, not the other way around, once again establishing that actions truly speak louder than words.

Even the American legal system places more importance on actions than words. To begin, I will examine the difference between the two types of verbal contracts: a verbal contract not accompanied by action and a verbal contract accompanied by action. Then, I will examine the difference between verbal and signed contracts. If a dying mother verbally promises her first daughter, but not her second daughter, a platinum bracelet but does not give it to her first daughter before passing away, who should receive the bracelet?

Generally, if the two daughters cannot reconcile the issue between themselves, a judge would decide in favor of selling the item and dividing the earnings between the two daughters. On the other hand, if the mother promised the first daughter the bracelet and gave it to the first daughter before passing away, the judicial system would tend to adjudicate in favor of the first daughter. However, the American legal system has decided verbal contracts with or without action do not carry as much weight as signed contracts. Thus, the strongest type of contract is a signed contract. If the mother's will indicates the first daughter's right to the platinum bracelet, there would be no issue for the court to decide. The first daughter's right to the bracelet would be upheld. Again, actions are utilized to substantiate words.

When Paul begins a debate class, he always emphasizes the importance of body language. Thus, he starts off with "confidence drills." These drills are nonverbal. He has students walk into the classroom with their backs straight, heads up, and arms to the side. Then they walk to the center of the room and look at their audience and smile. This is all done without a single word. His lesson here is that individuals are judged before anything comes out of their mouths. Therefore, it is important to look confident. People, whether we like it or not, do judge a book by its cover. Teachers need to remember that their students are sitting in judgment, too.

In the book *Blink*, Malcolm Gladwell discusses the work of psychologist Nalini Ambady. Ambady's study rated teacher effectiveness. First, students were shown ten seconds of a videotaped teacher (no sound). Then students were shown a five-second and then a two-second version (still no sound). The teacher received consistent ratings each time. The most surprising finding was that a student who had never been in a teacher's class would, after viewing a few seconds of videotape, rate a teacher the same as someone who had been in the teacher's class for a semester. This study demonstrates how accurate "thin slices" can be. First impressions do seem to matter.

I hope that someday the way we judge people will change. That we will look for the content of a person's character and for the substance of what he or she is saying. Who knows, people may finally hear you before they feel you. In the meantime, we all have to work hard to build more meaningful first impressions.

WHEN THEY GET IT

KENDAL SLOCUM

LOGAN HIGH SCHOOL

Morehouse College graduate

Mr. Lindsey was like a second father to me while I was coming of age and searching for meaning. My own father, although physically present, wasn't really emotionally available. My parents had gone through a nasty divorce just a few years prior to my joining the team, and forensics was about all I had to keep me sane. The first telephone encounter I had with Mr. Lindsey was during the summer between the end of my freshman and the beginning of my sophomore year at Logan High. He invited me to come to what was then the first year of a summer forensics institute. It consisted of him and a couple of coaches, and we'd work on speeches all summer for competition in the fall.

I didn't give a direct "no"; rather, I told him that I couldn't attend because I went to sleep the day before and when I woke up I was in Disneyland. His response initially was silence, but soon his laughter took over the phone. He told me years later that he swore I was crazy. But from there he persisted, and before long I was on the team and a fledgling relationship between us began.

On the days of tournaments, which often were on weekends, Mr. Lindsey personally drove a fellow competitor and me to and from each tournament site. Sometimes when other team members were riding the bus headed for the tournament, we were in his car laughing and kidding about things in our lives that we knew weren't really funny. That kind of nurturing support didn't go unnoticed even then, but its impact wouldn't have noticeable effects for me until years later.

He often took us to church, many times against my will, to either perform our speeches or to "get the holy ghost," as he jokingly put it. Mr. Lindsey never tried to convert any of his students but merely tried to expose us to different ideas. He saw us as individuals. He knew that what I needed at that period in my life was more than he had to give, but perhaps through support and exposure, I would make it through all right. The relationship wasn't always smooth, but it was what it needed to be when the time came.

Now, several years later, I remember the gentle, nurturing support that Mr. Lindsey gave me when my psyche was fragile. I can attribute my fortitude to the man who saw it in me before I knew what strength was. Mr. Lindsey taught me that it is not enough to be a person of ideas alone or one of constantly fading passions, but to find success in whatever you do, you must be whole in head, heart, and spirit.

THE FOURTH TRUTH

WRITERS BLOCK
BUT RARELY TACKLE

Writers Block but Rarely Tackle

Randy

> There is always a point in the writing of a piece
> when I sit in a room literally papered with false
> starts and cannot put one word after another and
> imagine I have suffered a small stroke.
>
> —*Joan Didion*

In seeking success, students sometimes get in their own way. They don't tackle opportunities without a nudge in the right direction. These students have never developed the work ethic they need to succeed. For them blockage becomes a part of life. This life of nudgelessness debilitates. The potential that lies within each student then remains dormant. This truth explores how a savvy teacher helps a student remove those mental blocks. The most familiar block, of course, plagues almost all young writers.

In Jason Rekulak's book *The Writer's Block*, he provides numerous examples of methods used by writers to jump-start their imaginations. Jack Kerouac wrote poetry after lighting a candle, extinguishing the candle when he had apparently lost all rhyme or reason. Truman Capote composed in bed. Bertolt Brecht preferred a pub. Ben Franklin liked to let his ideas bubble in the bathtub. The point, of course, is that successful writers find a way—a way that works for them. Endless ruminating, they soon discover, is seldom illuminating—a lesson learned by Nicolas Cage as the character Charlie Kaufman in the film *Adaptation*. Charlie (in voice-over) ruminates:

> To begin. To begin. How to start? I'm hungry. I should get coffee. Coffee would help me think. I should write something first, then reward myself with coffee. Coffee and a muffin. OK. So I need to establish the themes. Maybe banana-nut. That's a good muffin.

Forget muffins for a moment. Writer's block is just one part of a student's reluctance to tackle new things. Many distractions can take a young person's mind away from whatever task is at hand. On the "Imus in the Morning" show, historian Doris Kearns Goodwin recalled her love of baseball as a girl growing up in Brooklyn. In 1955 the only way she could listen to her beloved Brooklyn Dodgers play in the World Series was at school. Goodwin described what happened one afternoon in geography class:

> The teacher had no idea that the guys were sitting in the back with a transistor radio listening to the game. She had just asked the class, "What are the three products of Outer Mongolia?" And one good student said, "yaks, yurts, and yogurt." At which point a home run was hit. We all started clapping and this

stupid teacher said, "I'm so glad you love Outer Mongolia as much as I do."

Tommie and I want students to have a childhood. To live, as Dag Hammarskjöld said, "in the fleeting joy of existence." But we are concerned that too many students think—as Goodwin did—of their teachers as "stupid." The truth, though, is that teachers must help students develop a strong work ethic. A work ethic that allows each student to achieve his or her dreams, even if that dream is box seats at Fenway.

THE PERFECT GAME

Randy

If you chase perfection, you often catch
excellence.

—*William Fowble*

Psychologists have written extensively about the management of perfectionism. They express concern over "irrational beliefs." They worry that some students set unrealistically high goals. We should not be surprised by that. Our society is suffering from a sort of perfection craziness. In her book *Being Perfect*, Anna Quindlen said that finding out she was not the smartest girl in the world was like "carrying a backpack filled with bricks every single day." After a lifetime spent in the quest to lay her burden down, Quindlen realized that you confront the need to be perfect in the choices you make every day.

But how do you decide what choices, what goals are unrealistically high? In the book *Perfectionism*, Linda Kreger Silverman says, "The root of excellence is perfectionism." I agree. There seems to be a correlation between giftedness and perfectionism. That's why I have always set unrealistically high goals and why I have always treated all students as if they are gifted. The first step, though, is to solve the mystery of each child's giftedness.

There is something that is much more scarce, something finer far, something rarer than ability. It is the ability to recognize ability.

—Elbert Hubbard

I thought about this scarcity as I watched the film *Remember the Titans*. The film stars Denzel Washington as a football coach who struggles to integrate his high school team in Virginia in 1971. Black and white players take the field together for the first time. But the film is not so much about racism or football as it is about the human spirit. About respect. About a coach who finds the best in each of his young men. A coach who recognizes the ability that makes each player special. Washington's character tells his team that they must work hard enough to be "perfect." Anything less is unacceptable.

The team battles hardship after hardship to win every game and earn their way to the state championship. Only this time their opponents are just as good as Washington's team, maybe better. In the locker room at the half, Washington tells his players that win or lose, they should walk out of the stadium with their heads held high. The players have done their best, and that's all anybody can ask for.

The character Julius, a defensive end, says, "No it ain't, Coach. All due respect, you demanded more of us. You demanded perfection. Now I ain't saying I'm perfect 'cause I'm not. I ain't never gonna be. None of us are. But we have won every single game we have played till now. So this team is perfect. We stepped on the field that way tonight. So if it's all the same to you, Coach, that's the way we want to leave it."

When I told Tommie of my interest in this film, he shared how he had used it to motivate his team in 2001. His usual strategy was to show videotapes of former students performing their selections. But on the eight-hour bus drive to Long Beach for the state competition, Tommie set aside the final two hours for *Remember the Titans*. Tommie knew the truth in this film's message.

I won't tell you who wins. Why spoil the ending if you haven't seen the film? The point of this story, though, is to remind you how important it is to set high standards. No one wins all the time, of course. This lesson is taught in another football film, *Friday Night Lights*. The film, based on H. G. Bissinger's book about high school football in Texas, tells the story of the Permian Panthers' quest to win a state championship. In another memorable halftime speech, Permian's coach, Gary Gaines, explains to his team that perfect is not about the scoreboard. To him, it's not about winning. Gaines says,

> Being perfect is about being able to look your friends in the eye. And know that you didn't let them down because you told them the truth. And that truth is that you did everything that you could. There wasn't one more thing you could have done. Can you live in that moment? As best you can with clear eyes and love in your heart, with joy in your heart? If you can do that, gentlemen, then you're perfect.

We all need to understand what we are striving for as teachers, with love in our hearts. Students need to prepare themselves by working hard enough to make success possible. Perfect is the goal.

WHEN THEY GET IT

KATE VAN DEVENDER

ALBUQUERQUE ACADEMY

Northwestern University graduate, actress

I had always been bad at auditioning. I mean, really bad. I would step up to the front of the room to deliver a dramatic monologue, vomit up some gargled lines, and, realizing it wasn't going so well, stop blinking in hopes that the tears from my dry eyes would be mistaken for some Meryl Streep–like emotion.

It wasn't pretty.

This grew from being a minor inconvenience to a whopper-of-a-problem when I moved to New York to become a professional actor. I would try to dream up a way where I could skip the audition part and just get right to the opening night part. But wouldn't you know it, those Broadway people are picky.

There are *rules*, they would say. And I would explain that it was just the *audition* that made me nervous—that when I was performing onstage, in fact, I could be downright brilliant. Even my mother says so.

It's a cruel, cruel world when a mother's love can't get you a job.

Freudian analysis aside, I needed a remedy. Because all the world's a stage, and I was in the wings. Fast-forward through six years of a struggling career, and one day I found myself with the opportunity to audition for New York's top ten casting directors. It was an event set up by my agent, and it was big, very big.

I was waiting outside the audition room with twenty other nervous actors, and it hit me: I've been here before. This is exactly like competing in a high school speech tournament. I've prepared a piece, I'm competing for first place (in this case, a job), and there is a panel of judges evaluating my performance. I remembered that I used to be really good at this. In fact, I had won entire national competitions doing exactly this.

And wouldn't you know it, the panic drained away. It was that simple. I saw the situation for the first time without looking through a lens of fear, and I got it. This was no big deal. I felt relaxed and confident—so much so, in fact, that the nervous actor sitting next to me said, "You look like you're on vacation in the Bahamas or something. How are you doing that?"

My time slot came, and I walked into that audition room like I had walked into hundreds of rooms before—ready to compete. I remembered the tireless mantra of my speech coach: "You begin your performance the moment you walk into the room. Fill the space with your presence, command their attention. Smile, focus, and begin."

I kicked some butt in there. I did. And as I stepped back out of the room, my agent pulled me aside and said that I had knocked their socks off. With a huge grin on my face, I called my mother. "Finally, Mom," I said, "they think I'm brilliant, too."

LIFE'S TESTS ARE
NOT STANDARDIZED

Tommie

Education is what remains after one has
forgotten everything he learned in school.

—*Albert Einstein*

Oseola McCarty, a washerwoman who was forced by arthritis
to retire at the age of eighty-six, amassed $280,000 from a
life of hard work. That in itself is a remarkable feat. What touches
my heart, though, is that she gave $150,000 to a school that she
never even visited. Oseola taught us all a lesson—a lesson that has
nothing to do with standardized tests.

Yet I can see the lesson of her life to a smaller degree every day
in my classroom. One of the joys of teaching students from diverse
backgrounds is that I have come to know many types of cultural

experiences, foods, and customs—experiences I would never have known otherwise. Each student has something to contribute to my teaching. In addition to becoming aware of their diversity, I meet students with different skill levels. It then becomes my responsibility to provide those students not only with the skills that will improve their test-taking abilities but also with life skills. Developing the child as a whole is imperative if we are to make them contributors to society. Whereas administrations and school districts are focusing on high test scores, I try to teach my students that life's tests are not standardized. My student Andrew agrees.

ANDREW FONG
LOGAN HIGH SCHOOL

When does the college application process start? Most of us will say at the start of the senior year of high school. The honest procrastinator admits it starts the day before it's due. Some overzealous parents claim it starts sometime around the seventh grade. Few people realize, however, that it starts the second the student in question is born—if not before.

That isn't to say babies should learn how to bubble in an answer sheet before they learn how to walk, but it does say that the lessons that children must learn to get into the school of their choice should start as soon as possible.

After all, what does determine success in the world of college admission? Test scores? Grades? They must to a certain extent since students often ask me questions about them, hoping I'll spit out a gem like, "When in doubt, pick choice C," or "Mr. Lindsey reuses finals from previous years. Go look at those." Tests and grades are not the whole story, though. If the whole thing were simply about getting an A, my answer would be the same every time: cheat. Cheating doesn't get you far, however. Even if you

got into that number one college, your cheating would sooner or later be discovered, you would be kicked out, and the whole thing would be for naught. And, more important, cheating is wrong. Instead, grades and test scores matter only because they serve as a measure of how hard a person is willing to work academically. The important thing is the work, not some silly letter or number that no one will remember in a few years' time.

A strong work ethic, general honesty, and all those other things associated with one's character matter far more than any test or score; this applies not only to getting accepted into college but to all endeavors in life, whether it's applying for a job or trying to get a loan from the bank. Unlike your knowledge of analogies, however, your character is being tested all the time—starting the minute you are born. When you decide to watch reruns of "Friends" instead of studying for chemistry, you are choosing to be a lazy person. When you shoplift at the local Wal-Mart, you are choosing to be a dishonest person. Even when you choose to not push yourself during gym class because it's "too hard," you are choosing to be a quitter. People who are lazy, dishonest quitters never get far in any endeavor.

No one expects you to be perfect. We all slip up now and then, but people will still appreciate the effort. As Tom Lehrer puts it, "Life is like a sewer. What you get out of it depends on what you put into it."

Andrew understood why Oseola shared the fruits of her labor with others. For her, the answer was not about standardized tests. It was about valuing other people.

Oseola McCarty bound her ragged Bible with Scotch tape to keep Corinthians from falling out.

—*Rick Bragg, who interviewed Miss McCarty following her donation to the University of Southern Mississippi*

WHEN THEY GET IT

YIUVEN CHANG

LOGAN HIGH SCHOOL

I always had a respect for authority, and I have always appreciated what teachers had to offer, especially when they made their classes exciting. As I made the transition from junior high to high school, my respect for authority and teaching began to dwindle. The main reason was because no one really cared about me as a person. I was just another student among the four thousand students on this campus. No one wanted to hear my ideas, and most of the time, I got by in class by being quiet and respectful. In fact, I often found myself wondering what would be the best way for me to cut class and escape from this place I called hell. I called it hell because I was being tortured, forced to go to school, forced to listen to teachers' ideas and opinions, without anyone wanting to hear mine. I was able to get over on most of the teachers. It was simple. All I had to do was flash my charming smile and a little dash of bull, and I was able to get anything I wanted.

But one day this all came to a sudden halt. It happened about 5:30 in the evening, when I got a phone call at my job from Mr. Lindsey, of all people. I knew eventually this moment was going to happen, but I found myself paralyzed when it did. He was the one teacher I knew I couldn't get over. He asked me in that deep, intimidating voice of his, "Why haven't you been coming to my class?" I knew I couldn't feed him the same b.s. excuse I fed my other teachers because he would see right through it. So I told him the first thing that came to my mind—it was the truth. He immediately started to focus in on my attendance and me as a person. I remember him asking me what was wrong and why I didn't want to be in this environment.

I explained to him that a couple of teachers had completely embarrassed me in class. One thought that I was taking over the class with my questions, and the other was a teacher who yelled at me in front of the class because I came in from the bathroom late. These people completely turned me off and made my imaginary hell a reality. I told Mr. Lindsey that I didn't want to be here anymore. He took me to the principal's office, and I remember crying in front of the principal, and rather than the principal dealing with me, like the system does, he passed on helping me.

Mr. Lindsey saw that nothing was being done on the administrative level, literally. He went in and changed my classes. Though he knew that I would be behind in my classes, he still wanted me to finish strong. He began to take me under his wing. He gave me the confidence to finish the semester. The next year, I started taking a double load of classes. I was taking an English and chemistry class in addition to my regular course load. It was really hard work, and Mr. Lindsey would not let me breathe. We often had arguments about me completing the work. My theory was that it was going to get done; his theory was "let's get it done now." And in this situation, Mr. Lindsey always won. I went on to complete the semester and moved from a 2.0 GPA to a 3.87 at the semester. Now I am planning on seeking a military career, specifically in the field of satellite communications.

WORK IS CONTAGIOUS

Tommie

There is always a clue. —*Gil Grissom, "CSI"*

A CBS News article reported that "chemistry labs and criminal justice programs are what's cool on campus these days, as 'CSI' . . . and its spinoffs 'CSI: Miami' and 'CSI: NY' have created a whirlwind of interest in forensic sciences. Several colleges report long waiting lists for forensic science courses, and dozens of others are developing courses or entire programs in the science of crime fighting." It's quite evident that forensics science has become contagious, based solely on the popularity of particular television shows.

Unfortunately, in many classes across the country, another kind of forensics—speech and debate—have not caught on as well. Perhaps this is because many people have equated speech and debate with nerds or the wealthy upper class. Over the last sixteen years of teaching forensics, however, I've discovered it's something that can become contagious if supported by school administrators. I've watched a number of students and their siblings come through this program. It's not because they are nerds or are economically prosperous; it's because those families have a "clue." The clue they've uncovered is that a strong work ethic allows them to be the best that they can be.

PIERRE CLARK

LOGAN HIGH SCHOOL

Having been an excellent athlete all my life, I found it quite a challenge to even consider forensics as an option. My cousin, one of Mr. Lindsey's former students at the alternative high school, brought me to Room 408—a day I will forever remember. He introduced me to Mr. Lindsey, and I have to admit that he was an imposing figure. However, unlike many students, I wasn't afraid of him. I didn't know exactly what forensics was all about, but I had heard that it could be my ticket to college.

I was immediately given a selection to work on with my duo partner. Having the work ethic of an athlete, I knew that it took a great competitiveness to win. True to form, my partner and I won the first tournament I competed in. That's when I knew that this was something I wanted to be a part of. I was able to watch other competitors. I was able to express myself. I was able to understand what the concept of teamwork was all about. This was what I wanted to be involved in for my remaining years in high school. If this was going to get me into college, it didn't take a genius to figure out that I should be in forensics rather than on the football field. Consequently, I began to become more concerned about my grades, made the honor roll, was given opportunities to speak to community groups, and, most important, was able to gain pride in myself.

Pierre was able to reach heights that he never thought he could achieve. Not only did his grades improve, but he became a highly respected competitor on the forensics circuit. Sophomore year, he made it to the final round of the national tournament. For most students, this would have been the achievement of a lifetime, but for him, it wasn't enough. His junior year was probably the greatest year of his competitive life. I remember we tried to find the perfect selection, and after several false starts, we found it. *Life Is So Good*, by George Dawson, is about the life of an African-American man who learned to read at age ninety-eight. He wrote his autobiography after he reached the age of one hundred. Pierre "caught" this man's passion. If a ninety-eight-year-old man could learn to read and have the determination to write about his life, then Pierre, too, could work as hard to share something with others. Pierre's work ethic allowed him to become the national champion in dramatic interp. He was able to perform at the Horizon Sanctuary in Atlanta, fifty feet from where Martin Luther King Jr. preached at the Ebenezer Baptist Church. To end that remarkable year, he had the opportunity to perform on "The Oprah Winfrey Show." Pierre's hard work became an example for those who followed him in this program.

 WILLIAM WANG
LOGAN HIGH SCHOOL

Although I sometimes dreaded presenting during class, I looked forward to watching others perform. No doubt a majority of people started the year with lapses and mistakes, but as time progressed, everyone slowly crafted and toned their pieces. Sometimes it was amusing how much we knew of each other's performances, including the little details and gestures—more than we should have known of our own. Eventually, seeing so many people working hard and talking to themselves and their sections of walls after school (some yelling, some persuading), it was hard not to pick up their diligence. You wanted to have something more refined, something improved, not only for the coach but for other team members who were supporting you.

You may delay, but time will not. —*Ben Franklin*

Jean Kuei
Logan High School

I am a firm believer in prioritizing, attacking, and following up with tasks sooner than later. This is a habit that is not innate to most. It is a habit that must be learned and practiced. I have also found that tackling the hardest assignments first always leads to better results. There is more time for revisions, for feedback, and, most important, to focus on less tedious or difficult tasks. For example, in college and even in law school, I liked to work increased hours during the week in order for me to be able to relax and enjoy my weekends. Similarly, if you tackle the difficult tasks first, you will have more time to focus on less worrisome tasks and will find that you are more stress free.

The problem with failing to tackle writer's block or any other issue early is that you normally end up compounding the initial problem by continuing to procrastinate. If you wait until the night before to complete an assignment, you greatly increase the risk of not being able to complete it due to unexpected events, such as the printer running out of ink or the computer crashing.

I truly believe that if you do not procrastinate or take shortcuts, you will excel. Employers, colleagues, professors, and others will always notice and respect the individuals who possess a strong work ethic. They are more likely to trust those individuals with more complicated assignments and will grant them more ownership of their work.

A strong work ethic builds character and allows you to deal with the unexpected. The people with the strong work ethic are usually the people who end up being the nation's top political, social, and economic leaders, because people trust that when they are handed a task, they know how to get the job done.

In my case, I attribute my strong work ethic to my family and mentors, who instilled in me the value of hard work, dedication, and commitment to success. In our household and throughout my educational career, sitting on one's laurels was not allowed.

Who knows? Maybe someday, students will be filling classrooms across the country looking for different answers. Not the answers that lie in finding the causes of death, but rather, the answers found in clues about themselves. And through developing communication skills, those clues will lead them to a better understanding of humankind.

WHEN THEY GET IT

JAMIE WALKER

LOGAN HIGH SCHOOL

Howard University Ph.D. student in English, author

Mr. Lindsey always stood in front of his class. I can't remember him ever sitting. In his hand was always a note, a piece of paper listing our competition dates, a film manuscript, or a play.

"Stand up straight," he would say. "Emphasize certain words in your speech and use hand gestures wisely. Pause for effect if need be."

I always loved the pauses. Mr. Lindsey taught us natural pauses and to be cognizant of shifts in tonal quality. Indeed, we might as well have been taking music or voice lessons in his class, for every aspect of our instrument had to be honed and trained. Reading stacks of plays and piles of film manuscripts in his office, we learned the rhythms of everyday speech, as well as the rhythms of our characters. We learned how they walked, talked, laughed, loved, and cried. Indeed, we might not have known it at the time, but we were actually learning the rhythm of a strong work ethic—one that could only yield fruitful results with discipline, time, focus, and constant practice. Our teacher figured that if athletes, musicians, and ballplayers all practiced to hone and perfect their craft, then why shouldn't actors, orators, or public speakers?

All artists, regardless of their chosen fields, need to take time out of their busy schedules to hone and perfect their craft. And we learned that we were no exception.

"Get a good night's rest before your competition tomorrow," Mr. Lindsey would say. "Don't stay out and party all night." Stay healthy and eat properly. You don't want a sickness to prevent you from competing. Practice your speech in front of the mirror or in front of your friends. If necessary, record yourself at home on video and replay it to see what you can improve, which words you can emphasize, or where you can add natural pauses and hand gestures.

Know your character more than she knows herself. Don't be afraid of your own voice. Explore the entire range of your voice, complete in its resplendent beauty. Always aim to enlighten, not just to entertain. Touch people. Move your audience. Don't ever let them or your characters walk out unchanged.

End your speech with a bang—or quietly, with dignity and immaculate grace.

Read poetry to study the natural rhythms of everyday speech. Cry when something moves you, not just to move or "gain points" from the audience.

Admit all of your human foibles, both on- and offstage. If you mess up, that's OK. Keep going. Improve and strive to make whatever you just said or did ten times better.

If people in your audience ignore you, stay connected to those souls who are listening and need to hear what you have to say.

Remember to breathe.

Trust that you have moved and changed someone. Make everything that you do and every place you enter to speak a holy place. Always leave that space more holy than when you first came.

Remember that the world does not revolve around you but that you are, indeed, unique and have been chosen to bring something special and of great magnitude into the world.

Learn your fire. But don't scare other people with it. Anger does not sit or sell very well with the judges, your audience, or your colleagues.

Touch your pain, for only when you do so can you truly touch others.

Become a good listener. Study your competition and always give due praise. Treat your fellow competitor as your neighbor and your best friend. You will need each other when the going gets rough and when you both have wobbly knees.

Hold your head up high. You did not come this far to fail. Remember that we are all winners on the team called life and that each person's speech contributes to the well-being of the divine whole.

Be a team player.

Never get ahead of yourself—or your characters. Stay humble and always in the present moment.

Infuse your work with the spirit of life.

Lastly, let everything you do and say be both your meditation and your prayer. Thank those who have gone before you and provided you with the rich blueprint that you now stand upon, the blueprint that you will now revise and work to hone and perfect. Thank your teachers while they are still living. Thank them for believing in you (and your craft) when you did not even believe in yourself or this business. Remember that you are part of a continuum and that one day you, too, will pass on words like these.

No Buts or Shortcuts

Tommie

Be the matter big or small, do it well, or not at all.

—*Mrs. Dukes*

Over the years, my students have gone through many different, sometimes difficult, journeys in their lives. Many have made it, but a few have not been so fortunate. What I've always taught my forensics students is that there are no shortcuts in life. You have to take your time to get the job done well to get the best results. You may stumble, you may fall, but you have to pick yourself up and move forward in order to continue the journey.

I recall taking a trip with my friend Mrs. Dukes when she was 97 years old. (She is now 102.) She initially mentioned to me that she wanted me to take her back to Memphis to meet her cousin. I was excited because she was going to spend maybe the final years of her life with her last living relative. Mrs. Dukes is a very spry, sharp, and intelligent person. When she said she wanted to go to Memphis, I never thought in my wildest dreams that she wanted to travel by Greyhound bus.

I can remember it was an overcast day as we left Oakland and began our journey to Tennessee. Everything appeared to be set for a wonderful trip. Mrs. Dukes said that she had packed all we would need for the next four days. The first lunch consisted of Ritz crackers, cheddar cheese, and Safeway fried chicken, all neatly tucked away in a ten-by-fourteen-inch cloth suitcase. Not only was Mrs. Dukes happy to have me come along on the trip, but she was equally as happy that she was able pack breakfast, lunch, and dinner for four days. I remember sleeping for five or six hours, missing most of the short stops, and only waking up to the exchange of bus drivers. As I began to bite into my first Ritz cracker and cheese meal, I asked myself, "What in the heck am I doing?" Traveling on a Greyhound bus, with all the modes of transportation available, why didn't I convince Mrs. Dukes to choose another alternative? I guess it was just to make her happy.

As we reached Texas, I was often distracted from my sleep by the people who got on the bus. Some had peculiar smells, others became involved in arguments, and then some just wanted us to lend them an ear. At the rest stop, I escorted Mrs. Dukes off the bus. She was supported by her crutches. After we used the restrooms, but before we boarded the bus, I asked the driver when we would get to Memphis. He looked at me and said, "Son, first, you have to get through Texas."

It was two days since we'd left Oakland, and I thought we'd never get through Texas. On the third day, we finally crossed the border. By now, I had had my fill of chicken, cheese, and crackers. The bus ride was exhausting, but the journey for me was nothing compared to what it must have been for this ninety-seven-year-old woman who never complained about anything.

Well, we made it to Memphis, Tennessee. The only thing I could recall about Memphis was that Martin Luther King Jr. had been assassinated there. As we pulled up to the bus station, I got off first and Mrs. Dukes followed. She was able to get off the bus by herself, but as she tried to negotiate a step onto the curb, she fell. I immediately rushed over, but she bounced up quickly. I am and always have been amazed by the endurance and strength of this lady. Here we had traveled on this arduous journey for four days, and yet she had enough energy to pull herself to her feet.

Hours later, we reached the home of her cousin. It was quite a reunion. But after a year, Mrs. Dukes discovered that she could no longer live in Memphis, and she took the journey back home to Oakland all by herself. On a Greyhound bus.

I share the story of this journey with my students. The lesson is that no matter what the difficulties, no matter what obstacles and tasks you have to encounter on your way through life, you must always pick yourself up and move forward. There are no shortcuts in life. Sometimes the journey can be long and tedious—and it may be by bus—but in the end, the sacrifices make you a better person.

People are always blaming their circumstances for what they are. I don't believe in circumstances. The people who get on this world are the people who get up and look for the circumstances they want, and if they can't find them, they make them.

—*George Bernard Shaw*

WHEN THEY GET IT

PAUL BALDO

LOGAN HIGH SCHOOL

University of California, Santa Cruz, graduate

Mr. Lindsey, like my grandfather, was a man of few but very profound words. He told our class that each one of us is responsible for our own lives. Although this is a simple message, it is of great consequence. Each of our starting points in life are predetermined by many factors—socioeconomic status, family, culture—but where we end up is, for the most part, in our own hands. I have taken his words and made them into my own personal mantra: "my success or failure is in my own hands."

I no longer relegate my failures to what I have come to call "starting point" excuses. Doing that stunts personal growth. It is a difficult realization to accept. However, once I recognize that I am the captain of my own destiny, I can be free to accomplish my heart's desires. Prior to hearing this message, I would make excuses for my behavior. For example, when I would misbehave, I would claim it was a result of my parents' divorce and the lack of a father figure in my life. After my time with Mr. Lindsey, I took responsibility for my misbehaving. It is my fault that I would rather watch "The Simpsons" instead of doing my homework. His message made me realize that a private school education does not make people better; it's what they do with their lives that matters. Mr. Lindsey taught me that I am as good as anyone else so long as I work hard and stay dedicated to my education. He eliminated the burden of excuses.

Unmaking Mistakes

Tommie

Never interrupt your enemy when he is making a mistake.

—*Napoleon Bonaparte*

In the short-lived television show "Sports Night," the character Casey McCall, fearful that he might be losing the love of his life, says that he is going to follow Napoleon's two-step strategy at Waterloo: "Step one: just show up. Step two: see what happens."

In life, we all make mistakes; how we are able to deal with those mistakes depends on the character we have. Some mistakes, I've discovered—as Napoleon did—drive us into a kind of exile. Others, however, can be a learning experience. I've found that when working with adolescents, they often respond immaturely. Such responses test the patience of any teacher.

"HE HASN'T MADE ANY PROGRESS WITH HIS THEORIES RECENTLY, SO HE'S BEEN WORKING ON HIS RESEMBLANCE TO EINSTEIN."

Many of us expect instant gratification, but with young kids, *instant* isn't going to happen. Many kids, for example, do not know how to offer their thanks until they've gotten older and realized the impact that we had on their lives. As they move into adulthood, they become more appreciative of the time we've invested in them and what we've given them. I know a number of students that I've had confrontations with who have come back to express their appreciation for my caring. They finally understand that all of the direction and the advice were to allow them to move forward in life, to be contributors in their community. I feel that it is very important for me to command, rather than demand, respect in the classroom. On the other hand, I always make certain that students leave on a positive note after any scolding. That can be the beginning of unmaking mistakes. My former student Wayne is an excellent example of someone who realized his mistake, acknowledged it, and grew from the experience.

WAYNE HENRY
LOGAN HIGH SCHOOL

I've always known that in life no one is perfect. I was never a student who was successful in school. I got through school because Mr. Lindsey worked hard to tutor me and get me through the basic classes. In fact, I'm one of the few kids who went through Mr. Lindsey's forensics program but did not graduate from college. However, what I was taught through the speech and debate program was remarkable. I was very shy, and I would express myself through my music. I was the youngest in the family, and my mother always pampered me, so I expected things to always go my way. But I matured so much by being a part of the team.

I guess what I forgot, however, as I began to travel along my life journey, is that you should always remember the people who helped you get to where you are. When you begin to hurt those who are dear and close to you, sometimes it is very difficult to reestablish that relationship. Such was the case with Mr. Lindsey and myself. I had a disagreement with Mr. Lindsey, and I was afraid to tell him that I was wrong. I tried many times to get my courage and strength to the point where I could talk to him one on one, but I never could do it. Last year my mother died, and the only person I still had confidence in was the other person that I had lost in my life—Mr. Lindsey. I didn't have the nerve to approach him. The forgiving man that he is, he came to my mom's funeral and provided the comfort that allowed me to be forgiven and once again to reestablish a positive relationship. Mr. Lindsey had been my role model and support for many, many years, and I learned that I would never make that mistake again with anyone in my life who is as close and dear to me as he is.

Wayne went to nationals twice in humorous interpretation. He took second place in the state of California in expository speaking and in thematic interpretation. Even though he was not a strong college student, he had learned much by watching the other kids in the program. He not only improved his forensics skills as a student but also developed other talents that now benefit him as he manages his own business.

Experience is simply the name we give our own mistakes.

—*Oscar Wilde*

WHEN THEY GET IT

ALEXANDER TAN

LOGAN HIGH SCHOOL

I know that consistently working hard will reap good results in the end. Once I stopped trying to please everyone and trying to fit in, things started to fall into place. I didn't need to fit in anywhere or be everybody's friend—I could be my own person and would be no less than others. And when success comes, false friends just follow. I know this, and I've learned to keep my real friends close.

More recently, as a leader on the team, I have had so many people criticize my leadership ability. I realize that there will always be critics in all walks of life, and those who criticize the most are the ones who are detrimental to the team, trying to justify their position. Still, only a fool doesn't listen to criticism to find ways to improve. No one is perfect, but everyone can learn from their mistakes.

One of my biggest mistakes has been trying to mold myself to others' expectations to be accepted. I now realize that people should accept me for who I am. This newfound self-confidence is truly a gift—it allows me to take criticism without being discouraged and at the same time use it as a tool to improve. Leaders especially need to be confident in their convictions and remain steadfast in the face of adversity. At the same time, the best leaders must realize when they are wrong and know when to change.

I have devoted most of my life to my future. I have taken the most rigorous coursework in order to attend a good university. This, in turn, is supposed to get me a good job that offers me security, which is supposed to give me an opportunity to give back to my family. Forensics has been one of the very few activities that I do for myself, solely and selfishly, with little regard for my future. I do not plan on pursuing it in college, nor do I plan on majoring in speech or theater. But this activity has taught me far more about life than any of those honors and AP classes that are supposed to pave the road for the rest of my life.

WORKING SMART

Randy

If there are no stupid questions, then what kind
of questions do stupid people ask? Do they get
smart just in time to ask questions?

—*Scott Adams*

Students should never be treated as if they are stupid. The
teacher's challenge is to help them "get smart just in time."
Working smart is really about making good choices. Students
may feel that they already are bombarded with too many choices.
Do they get the regular iPod, the iPod mini, the iPod Photo, or
even the special edition iPod U2 autographed by the band? Alas,
the marketing genius behind this eight-hundred-pound music
gorilla will not guarantee that students live Apple-y ever after. But
choices—and how we, and they, think about them—do matter.

So let us think about some of those choices. If a kid's soccer ball bounces by our wistful stares, we gleefully sign the kid up for the school team and the local club. The kid has shown an inclination. Victory is ours. And another soccer mom is born. O frabjous day. Well, you can stop celebrating. Each choice made is limiting in its consequences. The time spent in practicing soccer is time not spent in exploring other interests. Now, we're not trying to discourage the next Mia Hamm or Freddy Adu, but too many students are forced to specialize too soon.

The education of a child should be a sampling process. If passion for a particular activity develops along the way, honor that. But gently prod the child to pursue other possibilities at the same time. Another possibility, after all, might be the smarter choice.

AMBER HALL
ALBUQUERQUE ACADEMY

I became a member of the speech team by accident; rather, it came about because I was a horrible debater. Because I was a new kid in school, my mom thought it would be a good idea for me to join the debate team and learn skills I'd be able to use for the rest of my life. Fortunately, I was a dismal failure. I ran into the speech coach in the cafeteria at one of the tournaments, and he encouraged me to stop by his office so we could chat about my possibilities on the speech team. Because I joined so late in the game, my debut as a dramatic interpretation competitor would be at the state tournament in Portales, New Mexico. I was still memorizing my piece on the bus on the ride up and barely survived three rounds of competition before I was weeded out. I was proud, though, that I made it through, knowing I'd do better next time.

And I did. State tournaments turned into national tournaments, and before I knew it, I was standing in front of large crowds of people portraying a variety of characters over the span of ten minutes. But what mattered was that I learned how to be comfortable in an unpredictable situation. As I stood on the stage, I didn't think about whether or not we'd get a trophy when it was all over, I just thought about doing my best at that particular moment. In my adult life, I continue to make all major decisions based on unpredictability.

I recently moved from New York City to Chapel Hill, North Carolina, having never visited the state before. My current job consists of working with the Latino immigrant population, and I am constantly required to be prepared to answer any number of odd questions and fulfill a variety of unusual requests that help the community adapt to living in the United States. I do it all with the utmost patience and grace because I want them to feel comfortable in a daily life that they cannot predict. There is a certain thrill, a real rush, to flying by the seat of your pants and praying that you end up with both feet on the ground. Through being a part of the speech team, I developed the ability to go blindly into a situation that I am completely unprepared for and make it look like fun.

Because it is.

When things go wrong, many students find it difficult to figure out what happened and what to do about their misfortune. They don't understand yet that working smart—for most people—usually requires a plan. Share with them the parable of the cow in the ditch. If you find a cow in the ditch, you must do three things. First, remove the cow from its precarious position. Second, find out how the cow got into the ditch. Third, do whatever you have to do to make sure the cow never gets in the ditch again.

In *Fortune* magazine, Anne Mulcahy, the CEO of Xerox, explained how she applies this parable to solve complicated problems: "The first thing is survival. The second thing is, figure out what happened. Learn from those lessons and make sure you've got a plan in place to recognize the signs, and never get there again."

This systematic approach grounds the student in common sense. And it makes it less likely that the student will waste time blaming others or floundering about. Working smart begins with assessment and reevaluation, followed by carefully thought-out action.

WHEN THEY GET IT

DAVID BALL

MILTON ACADEMY

Milton Academy teacher

A concrete cavern, the dimly lit high school auditorium in New York City sucked the confidence right out of me. I sat on a hard wooden seat—no padding here—frantically preparing for the debate tournament that had drawn hundreds of competitors from around the nation. My opponents, I feared, would be as merciless as the space.

As I fretted about my imminent humiliation, Randy posed an endless series of simple questions about the arguments that I was soon to present. I answered with relative ease, all the while wondering why Randy couldn't think of something a bit more sophisticated to help me stave off defeat. I was in need, really rather desperate need, and he was asking me to explain the arguments that I'd written just hours before. For an apparently great coach, this seemed like pretty rudimentary stuff. I didn't know it then, and I didn't understand it for a while thereafter, but Randy was beginning to teach me how to work smart.

For some reason, despite what I had assumed to be horrible preparation, I kept winning debate rounds. It seemed so improbable. My competitors were intelligent, articulate students from outstanding high schools. Still, there I was after the three-day slog, standing in the front of that soulless auditorium, receiving the first-place trophy.

What had I learned? Nothing, yet. Stunned by my own success, I promptly adopted strategies that ensured my subsequent failure. In preparation for a small local tournament the next weekend, I began typing up long lists of arguments for teammates, formatting those documents carefully, providing various sorts of commentary on my own lists. Then, believing that I needed to appear a bit more professional, champion debater that I was, I spent hours typing up my own cases.

I arrived at that little tournament with the best-looking cases I'd ever had. And then the losing began. There were twenty-five debaters at the tournament, many of them debating for the first time. I placed twenty-fourth. Each round deepened my humiliation. One opponent focused on a comparison involving a fire station and firefighters. I felt myself getting lost in the analogy, and with every move, I sank deeper into the intellectual quicksand. As I recall, the town burned down, all because of me.

In another round, my opponent decided that we needed to focus our discussion on a hypothetical common pasture and the hypothetical sheep that grazed there. I was accused of making the sheep starve. By the end of the round, they had. I don't know what we were supposed to be debating that day, but my positions produced fire and famine. Even I was horrified.

So what had gone wrong? Or more to the point, what had gone right just one week earlier? When Randy had peppered me with questions in that auditorium, he had forced me to articulate clear positions that a coach, a judge, or a competitor could understand. I was speaking, persuading, and defending—the very things that I would need to do in a debate round. Indeed, the last-minute nature of the preparation made it all the more effective.

When I spent hours that next week sitting at the computer, I was typing. I typed hard and I typed well, but when towns burned and sheep starved, I could only point in futility at the words on the page. I had worked diligently but foolishly, for I had not focused on the particular challenges inherent in a debate round. I could neither respond nor explain with the least bit of flexibility. It took that humiliation before Randy's lesson became crystal clear: know the task at hand. Choose a strategy that allows you to complete that task. Then execute. In short, work smart. Let the sheep live.

Practical Matters

Real Fluency. Real Fast.

Many students reluctantly speak in class because they find themselves mumbling and stumbling. They feel uncomfortable thinking and speaking on their feet. This drill helps them overcome that reluctance. If you have access to "CNN Headline News" in your classroom,* show a short segment to the students. Then turn off the television set and have the students stand and face the wall (for privacy). Urge the students to repeat what they have heard, combining the wording of the professional announcer with their own.

Repeating this exercise every day has three benefits: students increase their working vocabularies, their knowledge of current affairs, and their fluency as speakers. As a teacher, you will find fewer students chuckling in the back row like Homer Simpson: "it's funny because it isn't happening to me."

Please note that this drill works well at home. Parents and children can watch the news and improve their speaking skills together. For a change of pace, try different channels. I found that students enjoy ESPN's "SportsCenter." Avoid the Weather Channel. The meteorological jargon frustrates the students, and all of the numbers are hard to remember.

After all, as CNN continually reminds us, you have to learn to scrawl before you can run at the mouth.

I'm Bobble-head Blitzer. Let's get you updated.

In our top story, it's "splits for the Pitts." Jennifer Aniston, the former star of "Friends," and her husband, actor Brad

---

*You may find it more convenient to work from a script. At the end of this sidebar, I have adapted a CNN broadcast with a smidgeon of "The Daily Show" attitude stirred in for seasoning. The intent should always be to create a high-interest one-minute format that successfully engages students.

Pitt, are calling it quits. After much thoughtful, they say, consideration.

In other news, almost 100,000 people die each year from medical mistakes. At the pharmacy, twenty-six out of a hundred prescriptions are filled incorrectly. Four are potentially fatal. The American Medical Association asks, "But who's counting?" The AMA says it's committed to patient safety, but its top priority is protecting doctors from frivolous lawsuits and onerous judgments that drive them out of business. To which the the National Academy of Sciences' Institute of Medicine responds: "Our health care system is more than a decade behind other industries in basic safety. A fertile ground for lawsuits."

Anyone out there know the name of Jennifer Aniston's attorney?

This is Bobble-head Blitzer, CNN News, New York.

Drawing on
the Stories of Your Life

Randy

I think I've discovered the secret of life—you just
hang around until you get used to it.

—*Charles Schulz*

C harles Schulz, who created the beloved cartoon strip *Peanuts*, was invited to give a speech to a group of four hundred exceptional high school students. This special occasion provided Schulz an opportunity to offer advice that might be useful to these young people. He later said that he had difficulty coming up with an appropriate subject. After much soul-searching, he decided against discussing the need for dedication and hard work. He chose, instead, to break away from what he suspected were the trite recommendations the students had heard so many times before.

In his book *You Don't Look 35, Charlie Brown!*, Schulz shared what he said: "I am not one to give advice and always hesitated to do so with my own children, but tonight I am going to give some advice that is very important." He then told them to go home and begin asking their parents about their pasts. "Don't stop until you have learned something about your father's first job or your mother's early dreams. It will take energy, but it will be infinitely worthwhile, and it must be done now. It must be done before it is too late."

As we all know, though, not all students are good listeners. They have yet to understand that listening is more than hearing. Hearing is only an automatic reaction of the senses and nervous system. Listening takes effort—it's a voluntary act in which we use our higher mental processes. Some students think that listening is not a skill at all but something we do naturally. Unfortunately, we're not doing it very well. Studies show that we remember only about 25 percent of what we hear; in other words, we forget, ignore, distort, or misunderstand the great majority of incoming messages. So are we hard of hearing or hard of listening?

Evidently, one of my students was *listening* when I explained E. B. White's advice to young writers who want to improve: "Don't write about man. Write about *a* man." As the student prepared a college application essay, she informed me that she was describing the horrors of the 9/11 terrorist attack. I pointed out that members of the admissions committee might not find a rehash of "man's inhumanity to man" fresh or original, no matter how sincere her sentiments. The student insisted. And she was right. Why? Because she followed White's advice.

AMARIS SINGER
ALBUQUERQUE ACADEMY

My great-grandfather fled Poland to escape persecution. He escaped by riding through the night on a bicycle and by hiding in the swamps outside of Kraków, against the advice of others. His friends and family said over and over, "Don't go. Don't go."

But unlike the rest of my family, who did not survive, my great-grandfather made it to America. My great-grandfather passed on the importance of freedom to my grandfather, who passed it on to me. My grandfather used to tell me how fortunate I was by sheer accident of birth. But I know the rest of my life can be no accident. There must be a sense of purpose and a sense of gratitude. Both lessons I learned from my grandfather.

My grandfather was never looking for his fifteen minutes of fame. He was merely trying to make ends meet, and he did whatever he had to do to create a better life for his family. He fought to protect our country as a soldier in World War II. Then he went to the City University of New York on the GI Bill, and eventually, he became an engineer. But he never forgot the price that was paid by so many.

I thought about what it meant to be free when I was in New York City for my grandfather's funeral. As I sat and talked with relatives about how sweet and smart and wonderful my grandfather was, I couldn't help but think about how much his freedom meant to him. The last time I visited my grandfather's house, I sat in his garden. His favorite flower, alive and blossoming just weeks before, was now withered and dead. I cut the flower and took the seeds back to Albuquerque with me. Just to hold the seeds in my hand.

On September 11, 2001, I, along with millions of other Americans, watched the collapse of the World Trade Center. As I sat staring at the television screen, my father approached and reminded me that my grandfather had used his engineering degree well. Among his accomplishments, he designed the radio antennae atop the World Trade Center. That day in September, as I sat staring at the rubble, I saw it again: my grandfather's antennae, standing tall—a survivor of the devastation.

At age forty-two, Gilda Radner lost her battle with ovarian cancer. One of the original cast members of "Saturday Night Live," Radner was the sweetheart of Saturday nights. Her characters—the impertinent Roseanne Roseannadanna, the nerdy Lisa Loopner, and the misguided Emily Litella—made us fall in love with her. Shortly before her death, she wrote a personal account of her struggle with cancer. She told the truth with the same courage she brought to performing. Alan Zweibel, an "SNL" writer who published the memoir *Bunny Bunny* about their fourteen-year friendship, said, "She was accessible. She wasn't overly pretty. . . . It was just someone laying themselves out there saying, 'This is me. Like me. This is me. I'm gonna make you laugh now,' like a kid would."

As Radner's character Roseanne Roseannadanna would remind us, "It's always something." Students are well advised to search their memories for the "somethings" of their lives. These true stories make for the best writing and speaking. Readers and listeners are drawn to these stories. Students will soon learn that these examples are, as we used to say in graduate school, the strongest form of proof to the average person.

Sometimes a student may not have a relevant personal experience to share on a particular topic. What then? That's when he or she should turn to the true story of someone else. Students hear stories every day—from their parents, their teachers, their friends.

This book, in large part, is a collection of stories that illustrate specific principles. The key, of course, to any compelling story is in the details chosen to relate what happened.

 JASMINE BARNSLEY
ALBUQUERQUE ACADEMY

Grandma's was not an easy life. She grew up in a small adobe casita near an irrigation ditch in Tularosa, New Mexico, among pomegranates, quince trees, and five brothers and sisters. Each day from the moment she got home from school until she finally got her siblings into bed, she worked her hands raw. And yet she became her high school's first Hispanic valedictorian and with that honor came a full scholarship.

Unfortunately, though, her father became deathly ill and her family needed her more than ever. My grandma faced a difficult choice: to stay at home or to leave for college. So she made a promise to her father, a promise I was reminded of as I read the words of the poet Jimmy Santiago Baca: "Te prometi a ti y a todas las cosas vivas, que nunca te abandonaria" (I promised you and all living things, I would never abandon you).

That is a lesson I learned from my grandma, mi abuela—nunca te abandonaria.

Although the world is full of suffering, it is also full of the overcoming of it.

—*Helen Keller*

WHEN THEY GET IT

FREDERICK PUGH III

LOGAN HIGH SCHOOL

Morehouse University student

I met Mr. Lindsey in my senior year, and I initially felt as if he were someone I would have never encountered. I mean, in the schools I had attended previously, a black man coaching a nonathletic speech program was truly unheard of, and this was no small thing. I had attended some of the top schools of the region, but never before had I encountered a black man with such a wealth of knowledge and love of teaching. I remember transferring to his class; it was as if he could see right through to my very needs. As I sat in his class, I would often reflect on my favorite movie, *Glory*.

The movie revolved around the struggles of the Fifty-fourth Massachusetts Volunteer Regiment, which was the first black regular army regiment in the Civil War. The reason that this movie stood out in my mind is because it stressed unity, something I, along with many other black men, lacked. The Fifty-fourth was united in an effort to obtain equal rights and freedom for blacks everywhere. I would often see Mr. Lindsey as the leader of that unit, not only providing camaraderie and support but also taking individuals under his wing and garnering much-needed guidance and support. Mr. Lindsey never complained about the things he would do for me, and that was a plus because, as he knew, I hated to ask for favors. But asking was never required, as he was always there for mental support, stability, and focus.

Mr. Lindsey got me through my senior year. High school was a hard transition for me to make. I started at an elite white boarding school, then moved to a failing minority inner-city high school, and then to Logan. I moved three different places in four years. It seemed as if I was always on my own and had to learn both the streets and the country club to take care of myself. It was very tough letting anyone inside my web of coding.

Because of my constant moving and the instability it caused, I was forced to keep myself sheltered to protect myself from pain, ridicule, and misunderstanding. But through it all Mr. Lindsey was there, supplying me with faith and hope. When I was deciding to go to college, he was instrumental in helping to make my dream possible. He helped make all the necessary phone calls and provided key insight that allowed me to pick the school best suited for me.

Thanks to Mr. Lindsey, I did get to Morehouse. But I didn't uphold my end of the bargain. I strayed from my initial path of academic excellence and lost my scholarship by one-hundredth of a GPA point. I remember that Mr. Lindsey took the time to come all the way to Georgia and talk with the scholarship director, helping me to regain my scholarship and my way.

That way, however, still has many challenges. I lost a friend last year. He was very destitute and lonely and ended up committing suicide. I could almost understand his pain and grief. After his suicide, I again had a flashback to the movie *Glory*, this time to the end. It was at this point in the movie that the men of the Fifty-fourth were called on for a suicide mission. Everyone was confused and dazed, and many had to ponder the reasons why they were making the sacrifice.

As I called Mr. Lindsey and we discussed the situation, he helped give me the strength necessary not only to comfort myself but the others. It was from this strength that I gathered myself and was able to speak at my friend's memorial service. That is when I got it, Mr. Lindsey. When people are there to support you and provide comfort, it is your duty to do the same and hold these people near.

In the closing scene of *Glory*, the commander was shot and killed, and even though Denzel Washington hated him, he was able to pick up the flag and move on because it represented his freedom. Now, as is evident by this testimony, there is no hatred here. Mr. Lindsey has led me to glory through his continued support and encouragement. What he has bestowed upon me allows me to carry the flag to other young black men and pass it on to them.

PRACTICAL MATTERS
GRANDMA KNOWS BEST

> He's as safe as if he were in God's pocket.
>
> *—Grandma Amy*

While working in a Salem coffee shop during World War II, my grandma overheard the "God's pocket" expression used by a female customer. A few snippets of overheard conversation later, Grandma suspected that the woman had married a young soldier just before he shipped out, hoping to collect GI death benefits when the young man got killed in battle. Grandma said the woman had "sparkles" in her hair.

We live in a time when you can film or tape your grandma (or anyone else). You should record the stories of her life. Your recordings now will bless generations to come. If students want to undertake this project, teach them how to trigger memories in the interviewee, memories to transcribe into a permanent written record. I would remind them of E. L. Doctorow's advice: "good writing is supposed to evoke sensation in the reader—not the fact that it's raining but the feeling of being rained upon."

I often shared with students how I helped Grandma recall the details of her life. In one taping session, I asked Grandma to tell me her feelings when my father left home to fight in the war. She said she didn't remember. Telling students of the following conversation always proved useful as an example of what to say next.

ME: Grandma, didn't Dad fight in the Pacific?
GRANDMA: That's right.
M: Did he ever make it to Japan?
G: Yes. He brought me a kimono.
M: Then he must have been there after the bombing of Hiroshima. Did he say anything about the devastation?

G: I don't remember.

M: Weren't there still remnants of the dead?

G: I don't remember.

M: What about the buildings? There must have been massive destruction. Weren't some of the buildings made out of steel?

G: Yes, I remember now. He said, "The steel girders were broken as easily as matchsticks."

When I said the word *steel*, that was enough to trigger her memory. And I would tell the students that I had the first image needed to write a poem. Then I asked them what they thought would have happened if I had stopped questioning her when Grandma said she didn't remember. Later in our conversation, I would tell the students, Grandma recalled that Roosevelt died the day my father sailed, and I had the title for the poem. Then I would give students the assignment to interview someone special and write a poem based on that interview. I suggested that they do what I did for Grandma: print the poem on quality paper, frame it, and give it to her as a birthday gift.

Now I know that many teachers already use variations of this project in their classes. Properly preparing students to conduct interviews, though, should be the first step.

> An interview is frequently the course you chart between what you came in knowing and what you're finding out as it's happening.
>
> —*Terry Gross, host of "Fresh Air," National Public Radio*

"YES, I AGREE THAT MAN IS MASTER OF HIS OWN DESTINY, BUT SOMETIMES IT HELPS IF YOU PASS ALGEBRA."

THE FIFTH TRUTH

PAYING YOUR DO'S

Paying Your Do's

Randy

> I did something that no young Irishman should ever do. I began to ask myself, what is the meaning of it all?
>
> —*Frank McCourt*

In a commencement address delivered at Connecticut College, McCourt explained how he came to change his life for the better. Although he didn't have a high school diploma, McCourt managed to talk his way into New York University. Now, no one knew that McCourt would go on to teach high school English for thirty years in the New York public schools. No one knew that he would someday write *Angela's Ashes* and win a Pulitzer Prize. On the day that McCourt walked into the admissions office of NYU, he was just a young lad who desperately wanted to get into college.

McCourt informed a dean who happened to be passing by the admissions office that he—McCourt—was "very intelligent."

Having a bit o' the Irishman in me, I recognize blarney when I hear it. But that's not the point of retelling McCourt's story. His exceptional journey through life reminds us of how improbable that journey was. Unlike McCourt, most students do not have the self-confidence to do what it takes to change their lives on their own. Furthermore, they don't know what to do, even if the belief is there. Life is not as simple as it once seemed.

I always do everything right. I never do anything wrong. I'm the Romper Room Do Bee, a Do Bee all day long.

—Do Bee, "Romper Room"

If you were a child growing up in the 1950s (and years later in some areas), chances are you spent time with a "Romper Room" television teacher. Most children found the singing and dancing of the slightly deranged hostess mesmerizing. And there was plenty of moralizing about manners and conduct from Do Bee. The fortunate child had a Romper Room School "Be a Do Bee, Don't Be a Don't Bee" diploma on the bedroom wall. What the show forgot to celebrate is what happens to the child upon graduating to a real school. One regular viewer of the show said, "What they didn't tell you about was the random attacks by bullies, and the injustice of our school system. When I finally became old enough to go to a real school, I learned that bullies *do* have friends, and teachers can get away with punishing the innocent."

Since the show began some fifty years ago, much has changed. Popular culture has moved from Do Bees to do-rags. Still, a real school can be a fun place for learning. The number of slightly more deranged teachers, though, has increased. Budget cuts mean less singing and dancing. And danger does lurk in the corners.

Students soon learn that success exacts a price. You can't simply wander the halls like some meander-thal. This fifth and final truth focuses on what students should be doing if they want to succeed. They are the seven *ings* that can make a difference.

LOVING

Randy

If love is the answer, could you rephrase the question?

—*Lily Tomlin*

I suspect that Lily Tomlin was only half kidding. What we love and why can be perplexing. For our discussion here, we are talking about the passion that we hope students will have for learning new things. On the popular television show "The Apprentice," a recurring theme from the Donald is to love what you do. Too many students are just going through the motions in school. The mistake that many of them make is in believing that they have to love everything about what they do. That's an unrealistic expectation. Still, no passion, no joy.

KATE VAN DEVENDER
ALBUQUERQUE ACADEMY

Two years ago, my father gave the eulogy at my grandfather's funeral. I had not known my grandfather well: the Parkinson's disease from which he had suffered made it difficult for him to speak. I knew, though, that he was a master mechanic, and I knew that he often spent hours fixing things around the house. At the funeral, my father held up homemade tools that my grandfather had invented. One was an opener for Mason jars, another removed grease caps from a car. His last invention was a stand to help him put on his shoes when the Parkinson's disease made dressing a chore. From my grandfather, my father learned about the importance of each moment, each new discovery. I learned that you have to love what you do in each one of those moments. As my father explained, my grandfather was not a work-a-holic but a work-a-philic. He loved to work, and he shared that love.

But how do you get people to love what they do? More and more corporations are being persuaded that they need more laughter in the workplace. We need to persuade teachers that the same is true for the classroom. That doesn't mean that every teacher should be a stand-up comedian. "Seinfeld" was funny as a show about nothing. A semester of class meetings about nothing would not be that amusing. The goal, after all, should not be to tell jokes. Sometimes, it's simply a matter of creating an environment in which students are given permission to chuckle or chortle or even cackle. And, it turns out, it's good for you.

Loretta LaRoche, a humor consultant who has appeared on PBS, said that healthy people laugh some 100 to 400 times a day.

Syndicated columnist John Leo did the math on what this would mean. Yukking it up at this recommended peak capacity for seventeen minutes a day would be awesome: 24 times an hour, 384 times a day, 2,688 times a week, 139,776 times a year.

Laughter, of course, comes in many guises. Students should learn about the effectiveness of self-effacing humor. The ability to laugh at yourself endears you to others. The excerpt from Reah Johnson's oratory demonstrates how self-effacing humor combined with good writing strengthens the message in her speech.

REAH JOHNSON
ALBUQUERQUE ACADEMY

Sunday, October 15. I am at the mall with a mission. No, not jeans, ice cream, CDs, or cute boys. I am there to figure out the next four years of my academic life. Hundreds of booths are set up, each with eager college representatives passing out pamphlets, pinpointing information, and propagandizing anything pertaining to their school. It was the college fair, but fair it wasn't. Some booths couldn't attract a single soul.

Being the clueless person that I am, I must have picked up a hundred pamphlets. It was at the end of my trek, though, when away from the mainstream, I noticed *the* booth. Crowded with so many teens that I initially thought, "Must be a party school." I had to see for myself. Fighting through mobs of teenage girls and their mothers, I squinted to make out the university's name. "Clinique Bonus Time." Not a renowned university, but a universally known cosmetics line.

Instead of learning about, say, the University of Michigan application process, the girls had chosen to learn about the application of Sheer Sable blush. It shouldn't come as a surprise, then, that media researcher Jean Kilbourne tells us the number one wish for girls ages eleven to seventeen is to be on their high school speech team. You don't believe me, do you? Actually, what they really want has nothing to do with matters academic. They just want to be thinner. And, naturally, the number one wish for boys is to have a girlfriend who's well informed. Did I say well informed? I meant well formed.

A recent survey revealed that twelve-year-olds could name 5.2 alcoholic beverages but only 4.8 presidents. A third of high school students didn't know the United States had ever been in a war with Vietnam. Twenty-six percent of high school graduates couldn't identify Mexico on a map. And if you really want to be shocked, I could share with you my SAT scores. But then I would begin to cry and my new Clinique mascara would start to run.

According to author Steve Allen, Americans are suffering from a mental incapacitation, and he's not talking only about teenage boys and girls. To be blunt, too many of us have become what Mencken refers to as the *Boobus americanus*, a bird too ignorant to know which way to fly. Well, it's time to wake up and fly right.

Finally, students must learn that the love they have for what they do should not be at the expense of others. Passion without compassion is meaningless.

Life's most urgent question is, what are you doing for others?

—*Martin Luther King Jr.*

When They Get It

Andrew Fong

Logan High School

Harvard University student

I think I understood it better the second time around. The first time wasn't really the first. There were a few before that and perhaps even more after. Some I remember, and some I don't. It's one big blurry affectionate mess right now.

There is, however, a distinct second time—no doubt, perhaps, because it occurred quite recently. I had returned from another semester on the other side of the country. I was revisiting my high school haunts and decided to stop by 408. As I stepped into the room, I received a few waves and hugs. However, what struck me was the sheer number of people I just didn't recognize. There were still a few people who had been in the program when I had been in it, but they were underclassmen back then. Now they were talking about graduation and college. In a year or two, they, too, would be gone, and my semiannual visit to 408 would reveal an entire room of unfamiliar faces.

What had tapped me lightly on the shoulder several times before now struck me in the face. I celebrate my four years with James Logan Forensics not because we won Random Tournament X or were recognized for Miscellaneous Achievement Y. I loved those years because Winston wore a green suit, Marlon and I carried a stuffed raccoon and Vienna sausage in our debate tubs, and Bean made flip books of stick figures doing kung fu. I loved those years because I could count on Gerardo to dance in class, Amy to make snide remarks about stealing ketchup packets from McDonald's, and William to clench his fists when I called him Willy. I didn't love the program. I loved the people. Megan. Jay. Nikki. Mike. Teresa. Forensics became my extended family, and at the center of it all sat Mr. Lindsey, at a desk in the middle of the room, with a bottle of water and a stapler.

As I walked back into 408, I found some solace in the fact that Mr. Lindsey was still there even if the students surrounding him were different. It must be hard to try to be a father figure for the hundreds of students passing through the program only to see them disappear after four years. It's like having a child move out of the house every single year. And I think I understand how the yearning for days long past and students long gone can eventually wear someone down and push him to bask in the warmth of fond familiar memories.

I'm sitting here by the dorm window, looking out at the snow gently drifting down. It's a beautiful thing and it still strikes me as odd that the people here who see it every year don't appreciate it as much. How many times does the first snow of the season fall? How many times does the sun rise during your lifetime? How many times do you hug someone and feel as if nothing is wrong with the world? There are a thousand miracles a day—a multitude of things that happen without us paying them much thought, but every once in a while, we stop and go, "Wow, that was amazing." Or at least I hope we do. In any case, my four years with the program were amazing, and Mr. Lindsey was a huge part of it. When he leaves 408 and the sun rises for the last time, the time I spent there will be little more than a memory.

But it'll be a very fond memory.

Associating

Randy

Nothing, in my opinion, is more deserving of
our attention than the intellectual and moral
associations of America.

—Alexis de Tocqueville

In the 1800s, the French historian Alexis de Tocqueville wrote
that Americans constantly form associations. He recognized our
need to pursue in common the object of our common desires. The
common desires of most teenagers, unfortunately, would cause de
Tocqueville to blanch. In fact, it must seem to some parents as if
the wrong crowd is the only crowd. They have a right to be concerned. A University of Minnesota study concluded that hanging
out with friends was the biggest predictor of risky behavior.

When I first started coaching, I would hold "information"
meetings for parents who might want to know more about speech

and debate, who might want to ask questions about the value of our little subculture. I concluded each meeting with this question: "Would you rather have your child spend supervised weekends in an activity that emphasizes the intellect or unsupervised weekends dilly-dallying at the Dairy Queen?"

Choices do matter. Students need to understand the power of association. A teacher can structure assignments or activities to make good things happen in groups. Students must be led to the realization that they want to be around people they respect. People they want to be like.

Eric Fogel
Logan High School

Mr. Lindsey's classroom was magical. We would be surrounded by incredible people. One student would be imitating Malcolm X in a dramatic interpretation, another student would be practicing a speech on the probability for peace in the Middle East, an assistant coach from San Francisco State would be talking to a group of debaters about philosophy and the state of nature. Not only did I overcome my fear of speaking, but Mr. Lindsey could not get me to shut up! You couldn't help it in such a magical place.

Every person is a new door, opening up into other worlds.

—*John Guare*

MARK WOODHEAD
LOGAN HIGH SCHOOL

Not long after the state championship awards ceremony, the elation racing through my body quickly disappeared. I had received a phone call. I was staring face to face with the reality that I had lost someone very dear to me. The loss was unexpected; I could feel nothing but despair, anguish, and anger. How could something so horrible happen on perhaps the greatest day I had had all year? I was lost and beside myself. I cried but had no shoulder to cry on. That is, until I saw Mr. Lindsey. He knew me too well not to recognize that I had been visibly shaken by something serious. He took me aside, and after gathering myself, I told him what had happened. We sat somberly and talked, as if the world had stopped, while all the students were already on the bus. There isn't much that a person can say or do to make you feel better when you lose someone, but there are certain people who can help just by being there. Mr. Lindsey is one of those people. He was like a father to me, through the thick and thin, and for that, I loved him as if I were his son.

On the long ride home, I slumped down in my cramped school bus seat and had time for some serious reflection. I realized that this activity (forensics) that we all do isn't about all those shiny trophies or even winning the state championship. When I think back to my time competing on the team, I don't even remember how I placed at this tournament or that one. What I do remember are all the people who shaped my life: conversations with Lindsey at Denny's, long hours sitting with the team waiting for postings, getting the van lost in Chicago, or all the other little stories that stay with me. After all, it is in these ordinary day-to-day encounters that we all get a chance to know each other. These experiences are the ties that ignore all the individual accolades and bind together the individuals. The feelings of companionship, trust, and care take their roots in Room 408 and are what makes this *team* a family, the James Logan Forensics Family. They say you don't know what you've got until it's gone; on the contrary, if you really know what you had, it will always stay with you.

Lean upon me, I'll lean upon you, we'll be okay.

—Dave Matthews ("#34")

 NATHAN FEINGERSH
LOGAN HIGH SCHOOL

We had a student who I'll call D to protect his hard-core image. D was always mean to little N (that's me), but at that culminating oh-so-important forensics competition, following the proclamation of Logan's victory, D broke down in quiet sobs before N's trepid, gaping stare. With more than a dozen others, D let the tears roll freely as he embraced his teammates, including, eventually, me. What initially struck me as an onslaught of awkwardly excessive emotion suddenly opened my eyes to what I was really a part of—a family, a motherless multicultural family with Mr. Lindsey as our father and me as the immature brother. Although we competed individually, forensics became an opportunity to see what we could achieve collectively.

Trophies felt good in the hand, but in the end, all the pounds of plastic and metal don't amount to a fraction of what that family was worth. My four-year high school experience began with a love of forensics, but it ended with a sense of belonging and a deeper appreciation for my teammates and Mr. Lindsey, because without those relationships, I don't know what kind of guy I'd be, but I doubt I'd like me half as much.

Life is to be fortified by many friendships. To love and be loved is the greatest happiness of existence.

—*Walter Winchell*

WHEN THEY GET IT

VICTOR MAOG

LOGAN HIGH SCHOOL

National Endowment for the Arts/Theatre Communications Group Career Development Program for Directors recipient

I was up late one night in the parking lot of our motel in Reno. Most everyone, prepared for the next day's forensics competition, had gone to sleep. Not having rehearsed prior to that evening, I seemed to be living, instead of merely performing, Christopher Durang's *The Actor's Nightmare*. In the morning, Mr. Lindsey asked if I had been the one up until all hours. As he had surely heard my passionate parking lot intonations, I nodded. "When the curtain goes up, you're always ready," he said. And in that moment, I started to understand his belief and practice of faith.

My finances being what they were, Mr. Lindsey had subsidized my room, board, and tournament fees, in exchange for coaching members of the team. He surely had reached into his own pockets to help many others. Being the last-minute, midnight actor that I was, he wasn't exactly banking on an exemplary role model. But his belief in me resulted in my firm commitment to bring out the best in his other students. Sometimes the pieces I coached failed miserably, and on occasion, they placed higher than my own work. Whatever the outcome, I knew from him to set the standard high and know that it would be met and exceeded.

On the bus to Nevada rode what seemed to be the most confusing mixture of Logan High's population; we were all the John Hughes film archetypes gone awry. Each student had a competitive text, such as *The Actor's Nightmare*, but in the cramped corners of institutional vehicles and dreary motel rooms, our personal texts—our familial, cultural, socioeconomic backgrounds—collided and developed into a community, with aims to get through this moment of zits and exams and, perhaps, a deepened resiliency for and understanding of one's place in the world. Of course, fifteen years later, the lesson seems so crystal clear. On that bus, I didn't care about the multiplicity of races or the marginalized voice but rather about the loftier pursuit of who would go in on the two-for-one Big Mac deal. In my gut, I knew something to be right.

I learned from Mr. Lindsey the power of identifying and cultivating possibility in others. And through this series of tournaments, bus rides, cross-cultural summits, and personal investment, individuals had the opportunity to discover and build upon their own capacities.

Knowing someone believes in you is a powerful thing.

ATTENDING

Randy

You specialize in something until one day you find
it is specializing in you.

—Arthur Miller

When playwright Arthur Miller died at age eighty-nine, many
voices were heard. The tabloid journalists tittle-tattled of
his tumultuous marriage to Marilyn Monroe. The civil libertar-
ians praised his courage in refusing to testify during the era of
McCarthyism. But James Lipton, host of "Inside the Actors Stu-
dio," captured the essence of the man. Lipton thought of Miller
as an existentialist, a man who took on an indifferent universe.
Miller, Lipton said, "was engaged every minute of his life, engaged
with every word he wrote."

The unforgettable characters created by Miller were over-
whelmed by their lives. This must not be the fate of our students.

The battle to change that fate begins with engagement. Now we're not talking about the famous Woody Allen quip "90 percent of life is showing up." We are, instead, discussing the importance of attending to details. Purposeful effort. Dave Pelz, one of the world's best golf instructors, tells his pupils, "Practice doesn't make perfect. Practice makes permanent. Perfect practice makes perfect." This is a lesson all students need to learn. Phil and Tiger and Vijay don't go to the driving range just to whack away at golf balls. They have swing keys and precise targets for every shot. Left to their own devices, students, on the other hand, are likely to make the same mistakes over and over. If we help them to understand, instead, the need for purposeful effort, then remarkable growth is possible.

Tom Woodhead
Logan High School

Debate was all about planning, work, and strategy. The "thrill of the hunt." It was an incredibly challenging game of the mind. I had played many different sports, board games, video games, and social games, but nothing gave me the feeling of self-confidence that winning with my mind gave me. After all, we *are* what goes on in our heads. Winning with your mind is like elevating your soul. While it was this kind of all-consuming competition that hooked me into debate, other things showed me the importance of the activity.

The first and most notable element of the education I received during debate was the powerful set of critical thinking tools I honed and wielded with ease. These gave me an immeasurable advantage in most any social science or literature class, as well as a healthy skepticism that made science all the more intuitive. This critical ability was my fallback and my strength through the most

AS SMART AS HE WAS, ALBERT EINSTEIN COULD
NOT FIGURE OUT HOW TO HANDLE THOSE TRICKY
BOUNCES AT THIRD BASE.

difficult of university classes. Debate fostered a litany of other
attributes in me, including but not limited to research ability, writing skills, and knowledge of current events, philosophy, politics,
economics, sociology, and history. In fact, I was so impressed with
the things I had taken away from debate that I decided this activity was more important educationally than any other influence in
my life. It is no surprise then that I have dedicated my recent life to
coaching this magnificent activity for the very same person who
made it possible for me to do it, Tommie Lindsey.

Miller may be best remembered for his play *Death of a Sales-
man*. His protagonist, Willy Loman, is an Everyman, someone
who sacrifices everything to be well liked. Students must learn—
as Willy never did—what and when to sacrifice. Willy just wanted
to matter. Students must discover what matters. Speaking to her
sons, Willy's wife cries out, "Attention must be paid!" Listen.

When They Get It

Sharahn Larue McClung

Albuquerque Academy

Carnegie Mellon graduate, actress, teacher, writer

The state finals, my senior year, my last chance to make a mark as a competitor, and I was on a mission. Though I had made steady progress since my first speech tournament, I had not yet won first place. Coming out of the semifinal round, I was seized by a competitive spirit and told myself that I was ready for anything and that trophy was mine.

In the final round, I found myself soaring along through my selection. I felt that the audience was with me. Then, that "anything" happened. Through a window in the back of the room a chicken emerged. Yes, a chicken. (Normally, I applaud alliances between state colleges and 4-H clubs; in this moment, however, I found no sympathy for the study of livestock.) As the chicken pecked its way through the audience, chuckles erupted into laughter, glances dispersed downward, and I was mortified. Suddenly, all I wanted in this moment was for everyone to keep listening to my words. Slowly, I regained the eye contact and the attention of my audience.

Then two minutes and thirty-five seconds later, a Domino's Pizza delivery man interrupted with an obligatory "Domino's, thirty minutes or your pizza's free!" Again, I thought, "Listen to my words," and again, I pulled the distracted audience's gaze back to me. (I also attracted the focus of the confused delivery guy, who spent the better part of the round standing in the doorway, steaming pizza in hand.) The round ended and all I could think was, "Kiss the championship good-bye, and at least no one will remember the chicken."

Hours later, I sat on the bus, stunned for two reasons. One, I had already broken the little wreath off the top of my first-place trophy. And two, none of my ballots mentioned anything about the chicken or the pizza. One judge's critique only had "I felt like you were talking only to me" written on it.

In *Respect for Acting*, the late Uta Hagen wrote, "When all the work is done, every artist wants to communicate, no matter how much he may speak of 'art for art's sake,'" or, in my case, competition for the sake of a trophy. I never considered the simplicity of that statement. One want—I want them to listen to my words. One result—they listened. My need to compete was surpassed by my need to communicate, and everything else fell into place.

MENTORING

Randy

Too many mentors are really tormentors.

—*Eric Liu, panel moderator*

The moderator of our panel discussion was right, of course. As a member of the panel that evening, I was supposed to share what had made me a successful mentor. A large crowd of community leaders, after all, had gathered at New York City's Lincoln Center to celebrate Thank Your Mentor Day. In turn, each panel member spoke of a special relationship with a mentor, including the following:

Robert Abramson, director of the Dalcroze Institute at the Juilliard School

Father Gregory J. Boyle, the so-called homeboy priest, for his work with gang members

Tom Brown, a teacher of entrepreneurship in inner-city Washington, D.C.

Ivana Chubbuck, a Hollywood acting coach for Halle Berry, Charlize Theron, and others

Diane Dietz, an executive with Procter & Gamble (who has appeared on "The Apprentice")

First Sergeant Peter Hall, USMC, a former drillmaster for Officer Candidate School

Dick Monday, director of the Ringling Bros. and Barnum & Bailey Clown College

Such different folks from such vastly different backgrounds. A common thread in their stories, however, became apparent to me. Each mentor had succeeded, in no small part, because they, too, had had a successful mentor. And I was reminded again that mentors begat mentors.

But what makes for a good mentor? Although most of us would define a mentor as someone who gives another person help and advice over a period of time, there is much more to becoming an effective mentor than that. In his book *Guiding Lights: The People Who Lead Us Toward Our Purpose in Life*, Eric Liu describes the five characteristics of successful mentors:

First of all, these life-changing teachers receive before they transmit. That is, they are more than simply powerful communicators. They tune in to a learner's unique frequency of motivation and makeup, and only then do they send out the signals of their lesson. Second, they unblock and unlock their students, helping them move aside the inner obstacles—fear, doubt, shame, pride—that impede learning. Third, they zoom in and out, which is to say, they break down the subject to its basic elements and then use analogy and metaphor to connect the elements to something else the learners already know. Fourth, they know when to avoid direct instruction and to allow the invisible hands of a well-conceived, well-designed culture to do the teaching for them. And fifth, they know when to switch shoes, putting the learner in the role of the teacher. For often the best way to master something is to have them teach it to someone else.

If you want your students to develop into effective mentors, then you need to help them master all five of those characteristics. For me, "switching shoes" was always the true goal, though. I wanted every student to know what I knew. To walk in my shoes. To know not the facts alone but the *why* and the *how*. The facts were never enough. Emily Dickinson said of another poet, "She has the facts but not the phosphorescence." Too often we lose sight of the "phosphorescence" factor. Sparks must fly in the mentoring process. Excitement. Passion. Otherwise, when the student switches shoes and becomes the teacher, the emotion is lost in simple motion.

ADRIEL LUIS
LOGAN HIGH SCHOOL

Mr. Lindsey said it almost too nonchalantly. And I was annoyed. Leaning back against the puny swivel chair in his office, hands folded behind his head. "You're going to be a teacher."

I stared at him blankly. "No, I'm going to be a computer engineer." At that time, the possibility of me teaching didn't even register. I grew up as a son of a computer engineer from Berkeley, and I was adamant about becoming a computer engineer from Berkeley. And really, it pissed me off that Mr. Lindsey was dictating the direction of my own life—and that in conversations like this, he was never wrong.

"I'm never wrong."

"I'm going to be a computer engineer!"

"All right, I'm just saying . . ." He smugly shrugged and reached over to crunch on another saltine, immediately shattering half of it into crumbs sprinkled all over his sweater. Pshhh . . . slob . . .

Truly, it was on Logan's forensics team that I developed the notion of self-realization. Throughout all of high school, I scrambled for the relevance of forensics in my life. How was memorizing a ten-minute play, finding my interpretation of it, and performing it in front of an audience possibly going to help me in my future career?

Shortly into college I decided to pursue being a professional artist. More specifically, I am a performance poet. This job usually entails me writing and memorizing a three-minute poem, finding my interpretation of it, and performing it in front of an audience. Well duh, Mr. Lindsey.

I think he knew even then that my passion was more obvious than I allowed myself to make it. I have come to absolutely love teaching—fostering creative energy in youth. With all of the personal exploration that I have done throughout high school and college, I am finding myself coming full circle, discovering peace manifested in the relationship that we shared when I was that pissed-off computer engineer wannabe standing in his office. The dynamics between a mentor and a mentee construct the foundation of everything that I hold dear to me today.

In his book, Liu characterizes me as an autodidact: a self-taught teacher and mentor. Someone who teaches someone else "that kind of jerry-rigged, kick-the-jukebox-here-to-start-the-music kind of cognition." In other words, the autodidact finds a way, any way, that works for each individual student. Such freedom to experiment is not encouraged in most schools today. "Success in sameness" seems to be the current educational cant. Lots of facts, little phosphorescence. The anthropologist in me believes that fewer and fewer autodidactyls roam the earth these days. Standardization, not tiny brains, may doom us to early extinction.

I'd rather learn from one bird how to sing than teach ten thousand stars how not to dance.

—*E. E. Cummings*

WHEN THEY GET IT

DARSHAN PATEL

ALBUQUERQUE ACADEMY

Brown University student

Darshan joined the speech team in ninth grade. His mentor—Amaris, a fellow student—introduced him to the challenging world of current events. She taught him how to present his ideas in a clear and meaningful way.

As a form of behavior modification, the authors do not recommend pencil throwing. We do, however, applaud the mentor's commitment to Darshan's success. And Darshan's willingness to do whatever it took to improve himself. The payoff: the student became the teacher.

Every Monday she would be there waiting for me. Amaris, the Tyrant. Shuffling in, sitting me down, telling me that I do have hope in the world. Then I opened my mouth. Although I might have tortured her with my speeches more than I made her proud, she was still there. Every day. There are three things that I would never have known if I didn't know Amaris Singer: the first, that there's a country named Djibouti; the second, that the bestselling CD in Japan is the Prime Minister's *Best of Elvis*; and the third, that half of the world lives on less than $2 a day. Like most other people, though, I initially was afraid of public speaking. I was also a little afraid of Amaris. Why? She would throw pencils at me every time I would mess up. I didn't want to be the first person in my family to die from lead poisoning. But now it's what I do. I throw pencils at my very own novice speakers. I make sure I miss as they duck. I suspect that Amaris did the same.

At first, it was hard to convince my very traditional family about the merits of public speaking. For them, straight As and perhaps the chess team were the only things they could understand. My family never had enough money to send my sisters and me to play on sports teams. They would always send us to church instead. My mother, who suffers from the most severe type of arthritis and has to take more than a half dozen different kinds of pills every day just to function, had to at one point work multiple jobs just to make ends meet. So it hasn't been easy for any of us. But with a little help from my coach, I successfully introduced them to an entirely new world. My world. A gift that Amaris shares with me.

FOLLOWING

Randy

I must follow the people. Am I not their leader?

—*Benjamin Disraeli*

We spend far too much time in classrooms worrying about whether we are training good leaders. No one is self-made. We might be better advised, then, to worry about whether we are training good followers. This is not simply about preparing students to be part of a team. This is about preparing them for the realities of life. Not everyone can be the leader.

Students, therefore, must learn to become effective followers. In the *Harvard Business Review*, Robert E. Kelley described four essential qualities of effective followers. I have adapted his four business principles to what is needed in the classroom.

1. *Self-directed.* Effective student followers develop the ability to think for themselves.
2. *Committed.* These students are committed to what is best for the class. They support the purpose of what takes place each day.
3. *Competent.* These students set high standards for themselves. They are about improving their skills and abilities.
4. *Courageous.* They keep fellow students honest. These effective followers are never afraid to speak up if something is wrong.

Clearly, followers bear much responsibility for the success of any undertaking. And that is why—sometimes—the follower must take a stand. In her essay, Molly Dunn shares the power of an effective follower.

MOLLY DUNN

ALBUQUERQUE ACADEMY

When I was a fifth grader at S. Y. Jackson Elementary School, my best friend, Sarah, was the typical nerd. One day, when the teacher was out of the room for a while, the class bully decided it would be fun to lock Sarah out of the classroom. As her best friend, I could not stand by and let this happen. I stood outside, locked out of the classroom with her. Sarah was so hurt by the bully's actions that she was bawling. Then, one by one, my entire class came to stand outside with us.

The danger in the leader-follower relationship is the assumption that the leader's interpretation must dominate. If this assumption exists on the part of either the leader or the follower, creativity and problem solving become stifled.

—*Patsi Krakoff*

WHEN THEY GET IT

MICHAEL JOSHI

LOGAN HIGH SCHOOL

Harvard University student

I enjoy playing cards, but I also value them for another reason. I strongly believe that no one deserves respect; respect is something you must earn. And for some reason, I have always been one to appreciate earning the respect of my elders over that of my peers. Of course, this does not mean I do not appreciate the latter, but I feel that the former more often understands the value of being respectful. Coincidently, the better card players I have met are older than me. I try to follow their lead.

A very specific situation comes to mind. I was attending the California Youth Think Tank last summer, and the director of the camp, William Allen Young, came up to a group of us playing spades during a break (I told you I enjoy playing cards). He asked if any of us knew how to play bid whist. I had just been taught the week before by my speech and debate coach, Tommie Lindsey (who is responsible for my love of spades) and had yet to play a real game. However, I had been dealing myself hands to become familiar with bidding, and I really wanted to play. That evening, I sat down with Mr. Young and his partner in crime, Howard Ransom Jr. (they had played together often and could not help exhibiting confidence). Across from me was Milton Johnson III. I knew little about any of them, except that they were devoting their time to this think tank to improve the lives of kids like myself (by the end of the camp, I was more than convinced that they were outstanding individuals).

My partner and I were quiet, but I doubt he was as anxious as I was; I was the one out of place. By the time we had finished, we were all having a good time, and all three of them were noticeably impressed with me. Milton and I had won all five games, a couple of which I had taken control of myself. Yet there was a sense of camaraderie rather than division between the two teams. I began to feel very comfortable among my fellow players, despite being well outside their peer group. And I had accomplished this simply by being myself; to me, playing cards is playing cards, nothing more. There is not anything more satisfying to me than being respected for being myself and doing what I do.

I do not act abnormally to earn respect. I take the hand I have been dealt, and I stick with the strategy that feels right. I try to get good grades, accept leadership responsibilities on the forensics team, and act respectfully because *I* feel those things are important. However, I do recognize that other people watch me play cards, and for them I understand the importance of being the best role model possible. I believe, since I have been influenced by those before me, that we are responsible for teaching those who follow us. But do I teach them to pass the queen of spades? Go for the nil? Bid four-no? Maybe. Or maybe I teach them to arrange their own hands.

RISKING

Randy

Our doubts are traitors, and make us lose the
good we oft might win by fearing to attempt.

—William Shakespeare

My fifth grade English teacher was fearless. She actually believed that ten-year-olds could perform Shakespeare. Well, she put up a good front anyway. After she had cast us in "suitable" parts, she would read a few pages to us from the Bard. We were, then, to act out what we had just heard in our own words. I don't remember exactly, but I assume that it was a young person's version of the plays that she read. I say that because I think I understood most of what the characters said.

The highlight of the year for me was playing the lead in *Hamlet*. My teacher decided that we should subject the parents to our interpretation of this tragedy. Clearly, my teacher was prepared to "suffer the slings and arrows of outrageous fortune." During rehearsal I had the opportunity to leap from a chair into Ophelia's imaginary grave. You could tell it was her grave; the poor girl who portrayed Ophelia lay prostrate next to the chair that slid easily on the freshly waxed wooden floor. The reason I remember this scene so vividly is because I would leap with my feet spread slightly apart in an attempt to come as close as possible to Ophelia's now reddening ears.

I don't recall much about opening night. I had the distinct feeling, though, that the audience was unanimous in their agreement: I should "not to be."

All of this is to say that we should encourage students to be risk takers. Students need to understand, however, that if you take risks, you are going to lose sometimes. Many do not try, therefore, because they fear failure. You can't be on the playing field, in the school play, or in the orchestra if you aren't willing to take the risk of not succeeding. Daring to try something new is not always easy. Parents and teachers must be role models in risk taking. Supportive when things don't work out. And then there's the kicking and screaming. You do what you have to do. And you make sure you have a huge safety net.

> The person who risks nothing, does nothing, has nothing, is nothing, and becomes nothing. He may avoid suffering and sorrow, but he simply cannot learn and feel and change and grow and love and live.
>
> —*Leo F. Buscaglia*

David Lopez (coached by Lanny Naegelin) of San Antonio Churchill High School in Texas delivered one of my favorite oratories: "The Rhetoric of No." The speech highlighted the willingness of some people to risk everything in standing up for their beliefs. Lopez said this about his speech:

> I always felt that the speech's substantial appeal to audiences arose from its ability to draw from the simplest of words, from the word "no," these two powerful truths—that it takes courage to stand for "mighty opposites" as well as to respect those who do the same.

Of course, students aren't typically confronted by the same life choices as Socrates or Galileo or Rosa Parks. The risks for them are smaller, but they are real just the same. In that sense, students find themselves tested every day. In the choices they make. In the risks they take.

WHEN THEY GET IT

JEREMY MALLORY

ALBUQUERQUE ACADEMY

University of Chicago Law School student

Here Jeremy describes the risk he took in the final round as he attempted to win a national championship in extemp. His courage and creativity were rewarded.

Epiphanies often arrive over the subtitle "I hope my coach doesn't kill me."

The file on Prozac was a little thin. A handful of articles were in there and lay scattered through other files. To make matters worse, there wasn't a single political cartoon to be found, which eliminated the comfortable source of introductory material I had used for a long time. This was a recipe for a flat, boring speech bearing the hallmarks of the topics I found least inspiring: economics, medicine, and regulation. Whee.

Tucked into a file on health insurance (I think) was an article whose title I will never forget: "Boo! You're Dead!" The article compared the risks of undertaking various activities, culminating in the realization that the two days we had been drinking New York tap water for this tournament raised our risk of death by the same amount as if we had each smoked about twenty cigarettes.

By deciding to take a risk and "waste time" on a nontraditional introduction—fully against my coach's recommendations to tighten up my rambling intros—I ended up giving a speech that entertained me greatly, transforming a flat, beige topic into a vivid discussion of risk. At the time, however, I was ready to accept the fact that it might have gone over like lead paint.

I did not, thankfully, die, either from homicide or dihydrogen oxide poisoning. My coach had always repeated the mantra "It's exactly what we wanted" in the face of success and failure, victory and defeat. In that moment of panic when I realized, first, that I had a potential dozer of a speech on my hands and, second, that I could change that by taking an unanticipated risk and accepting the consequences where they lay, I learned in a deep sense what that mantra meant to me. Either way, it would be exactly what I wanted it to be (and I was very thankful to have a coach who would accept the consequences with me as what we wanted, rather than leaving me to reap alone what I sowed).

These surprise moments of panic are opportunities—exactly the ones we wanted—to show innovation by taking risk or to demonstrate strength by moving forward nevertheless. Just realizing that choice, then making it consciously, is an epiphany.

PERSISTING

Randy

That which we persist in doing becomes easier—
not that the nature of the task has changed, but
our ability to do so has increased.

—*Ralph Waldo Emerson*

To persist is not merely to survive. Now the struggle begins. In his book *Audition*, Michael Shurtleff says that Chekhov's play *Three Sisters* is not about three women on their way to Moscow. It's about "fighting like hell to get there."

Meaningful persistence requires more than stick-to-itiveness. The "fighting like hell" that takes place should include personal growth. In my first year as a speech coach, I knew little about how to prepare students to participate in the events offered. From my high school experience as a debater, I had vague notions of what was expected in that activity, but the different speech events remained largely a mystery. Before competing in a speech tournament, I called another coach to ask him about what a student should do to compete successfully in extemporaneous speaking. He said that the judges would award first place to the student who best answered the question. What question? I wondered. So I told my one student willing to enter the extemporaneous speaking competition to answer the question. She said, "OK," fearless kid that she was. She didn't bother to ask what question either.

Later I learned that students were given three topics to choose from, all in the form of a question. The student would then have thirty minutes to prepare a well-organized, well-evidenced seven-minute speech. Without notes.

In her opening round of competition, my student chose the following topic: "How can we better protect President Ford from assassination?"

The judge who heard her speech sought me out after the round. He then said those words—repeated many times over in subsequent years—that always sent chills up my spine. "Do you know what your student just did?" Evidently, my student entered the classroom and stated the question, "How can we better protect President Ford from assassination?" Next—after standing silently for several seconds—she said, "Well, we could put him on a motorcycle so that he could ride real fast through crowds. Thank you." And she left the room.

The judge chuckled as he told me that he had given her second place out of six extemporaneous speakers. His assessment: at least she answered the question. This young lady persisted, though, until she actually had something to say. As a state champion in oratory, she continued to fight to improve. But she had already answered the most important question: What are you willing to do to become all that you can be?

LeVar Eady

Logan High School

During high school Mr. Lindsey would always say, "LeVar, you have to work harder, practice more, and put everything into it." He had an uncanny ability to see when I was not living up to my full potential. He always inspired me to persevere and exceed my own expectations. It was during these times that I realized he was not just talking but teaching me invaluable life lessons. Most important, his benevolent spirit did not escape me when I left high school. During my freshman year at Morehouse College, I was having a hard time in some of my classes. I was seeing more than half the people in my major (biology) drop. They dropped because of how hard the classes were and because of the workload. This was a shock to me because in high school pretty much all my classes were easy and did not involve much studying on my part.

I honestly believe if it were not for the lessons of Mr. Lindsey, I probably would have changed my major as well. The result of changing my major would have put me in a position I really didn't want. I knew I just had to push on and give my all. The lesson that he taught me doesn't just apply only to class but to life. I know that I am better equipped for the real world as a result of Mr. Lindsey. The reason I know this is because there are always going to be trials and tribulations that people go through. So if you succumb to those adversities, you will never be anything or go anywhere. Helen Keller was right when she said, "Character cannot be developed in ease and quiet. Only through experience of trial and suffering can the soul be strengthened, ambition inspired, and success achieved." This sums up what I think Mr. Lindsey was trying to tell me all those years.

You may remember the story of Aron Ralston, the twenty-seven-year-old adventurer from Colorado. While hiking in April 2003, Ralston became trapped when an eight-hundred-pound boulder shifted, crushed his hand, and pinned him to a canyon wall. Trapped and facing certain death, he made a choice. To persist. To survive. Using a multitool, the climber amputated his right hand.

Later, at a press conference in a small room in Grand Junction, Colorado, Ralston went through the ordeal again. He described, in excruciating detail, the harrowing experience for all of the reporters that had gathered there. Ralston had become an international sensation. After the press conference, he returned to his hospital room with *Sports Illustrated* writer Rick Reilly. Reilly reports that Ralston made just one comment: "I wish I could have been funnier."

Fortunately, most students will never get trapped by a boulder. Nor are they likely to have to make life-and-death decisions. But they will face much adversity in their lives. Let's hope they choose to persist. Let's hope they face those moments with a sense of humor.

REAH JOHNSON
ALBUQUERQUE ACADEMY

The second-week assignment in our Effective Speaking class was to deliver a speech on the meaning of life—a difficult topic for even the most scholarly of theologians. But I found it particularly grueling as a female sophomore in a class of all seniors that, mind you, included two cocaptains of the boys' varsity soccer team.

The night before my speech, I stayed up until midnight going through revision after revision. Nothing was good enough! What if everyone would be able to tell that I had no clue what the mean-

"ARE YOU SURE
EINSTEIN STARTED THIS WAY?"

ing of life was? What if I looked totally stupid? How should I do my hair?

The next day, I walked to the front of the class, barely able to breathe. My hands shook as I held the speech in front of me. I was only through the second sentence when I thought to myself, "I hate this!" I had one of two options: undergo a triple bypass at the age of fifteen or let go of my fears and get through it. I opted for the latter, and boy did it feel good! After all, I may have been a measly sophomore, but none of the previous speakers had convinced me that they knew the meaning of life.

The combination of a brilliantly far-fetched speech assignment and an absolutely terrifying audience forced me to realize the power of staying cool. Of persisting. We will always encounter questions we don't know how to answer and uncomfortable occasions in the spotlight. But fortunately for us, our cool, our will to fight—these are always in our control. Too often we waste more energy agonizing under the fear of failure than it takes to just step up to the plate. We need to take deep breaths, project confidence, and, when we can, enjoy ourselves. Easier said than done? Obviously. But if we don't at least try, then we're setting ourselves up for failure. I still may not know the meaning of life, but I'm pretty sure it's not to make ourselves miserable.

When Austan Goolsbee walked through my classroom door, he announced that he wanted to be the best extemporaneous speaker in the nation. I asked him if he was willing to give a practice speech every day after school (this may not seem like much to ask, but forensics is not gymnastics). Most Milton Academy students at that time felt that they were too busy to give even one practice speech a week.

Austan said—in many more words—"no problem." And our two-year journey began. While listening to his early practice speeches, I would often find myself literally rolling on the floor with laughter. He would compare each topic—the economy of the former Soviet Union, the efforts to reduce school violence, the environmental policy of the United States—to an airplane taking off. Frequent flights of fancy. Few survivors.

But Austan was there every afternoon. He read. He wrote. He spoke. He improved. By the time he graduated, Austan became arguably the most successful high school extemporaneous speaker in the history of interscholastic competition. Winner of three individual national championships (two at Catholic Nationals and one at the National Forensic League Nationals), Austan persisted until he achieved his goal.

WHEN THEY GET IT

AUSTAN GOOLSBEE

MILTON ACADEMY

University of Chicago professor of economics

In high school I traveled a lot to speech tournaments, and whenever something went wrong, Randy McCutcheon (my coach) would always say, "Everything that happens is a break for us." At first, I viewed this as a message to keep a positive attitude. Ultimately, though, I decided there was something much deeper to it.

Once he and I were at an American Legion speaking contest in Alabama. It was the final event of a long year of contests whose prizes would, ultimately, end up paying a sizable share of my college tuition. The stakes being high enough, I remember feeling antsy. They put all the finalists up at a golf resort in Tuscaloosa, each in our own little cabana. Randy and I decided to go down to the pool to relax before the final round. We didn't have bathing suits, so we just waded around in our shorts and T-shirts. Anyway, we didn't keep track of time or I don't know what happened, and we suddenly realized the final round was starting in about thirty minutes, and we were soaking wet and needed to get back to the cabana and change and get down to the contest as fast as we could. We couldn't find a shuttle, so we ran across a large expanse of the golf course to get there.

Upon arriving, we discovered our luggage wasn't there yet (though fortunately, my suit was in the car downstairs). Yes, there were fancy bathrobes, but for dry underwear, we had to pull out the hair dryers and do it by hand. As I was standing there in a bathrobe drying my underwear with about fifteen minutes before we were supposed to be speaking, Randy told me, "Just remember that everything that happens is a break for us."

The thing was, I knew that he wasn't trying to cover up the stress of the situation. He believed it. And I did, too. He meant it. Back in those days, there was no Internet, so the only way to study a topic for speech was either to get a book from the library or to read all the newspapers and all the magazines every day and to clip the articles and put them in giant files. Since there are so many obscure topics, you were constantly afraid of talking about something you knew nothing about. It seemed so random. You had to get lucky. Randy would tell me that the only way around those fears was to prepare, and he told me to practice every day. So I did: reading, clipping, giving speech after speech. For a long time, I would complain to Randy that no one could possibly speak on the topics he would give me. They were too hard, too obscure, too whatever. Why couldn't we just give practice speeches on topics I knew about? But he wouldn't go for it.

Slowly, I began complaining less and learning more. One day he gave me a foreign policy topic about agricultural reform in Tanzania. I didn't know much about it, but I sat down and worked through it. After months of practice, I really didn't think much of it. When it was done, I remember thinking, "Wow, a year ago I wouldn't have been able to do that, but today I am." And just then, I finally understood that when Randy said, "Everything that happens is a break for us," he meant it quite literally, not as whitewash. If we could be the best-prepared people in the room, then we would be the best at thinking on our feet or adjusting to things that went wrong. Anything unusual that happened would be to our advantage. It really would be a break for us. For anyone who wasn't prepared, things like that would just seem like bad luck.

So when Randy and I were standing there drying our clothes with a hair dryer and he said this was really a break for us, I started laughing and I believed it. Looking back on it, maybe it was a bit of a stretch to cast having to dry my underwear ten minutes before the final speech and not getting a chance to prepare as a "break for us." Come to think of it, though, I do recall the room I spoke in that day being massively over-air-conditioned. Those toasty boxers felt pretty nice. I guess Randy was right all along.

Final Thoughts

Randy

It wasn't by accident that we made the most essential truth, Be the First Believer, the first truth. You must learn to believe in yourself. As a teacher. As a parent. Then you must pass that belief on. One child at a time. Your faith in yourself and others will be tested many times. The truths we offer in this book are there to inspire you, to make meeting each challenge joyful. Tommie and I truly believe that the life of a teacher can be joyful, but—as the student stories suggest—it is never easy.

I remember Lenny Bruce defining *obscenity* by comparing the gobs of money Zsa Zsa Gabor got paid to perform for a week in Las Vegas to the $6,000 average annual salary of teachers in Nevada. If Bruce were alive today, he might broaden his definition, and he still wouldn't be joking. Obscenity in education, it seems, has taken on additional meaning. In fact, we now have a fourth R: rudeness. Disrespect is rampant in most public schools. Some teachers spend half of each class period disciplining unruly children.

But failing behavior is just one bad trip on your "teaching vacation." Consider some of the other bad trips in store for you: Standardized tests that monopolize precious class time. Watered-down textbooks. Absent or hostile parents. Administrators who "rule" by convenience. Massive budget cuts. *Mr. Holland's Opus* may be just a DVD memory, but the malady lingers on. Is it any wonder that the annual turnover rate for teachers in America is 16 percent? Other professions have a turnover rate of 11 percent. Talk about "freakonomics."

Our editor thinks my writing style is occasionally "wacky." I take this as a compliment. General wackiness made it possible for me to survive twenty-seven years in the classroom. Wackiness prompted me to get up in the morning each day to fight the good fight. Tommie feels the same. He is proud to be described as "a nut with a mission."

After all, in the Preface to this book, Tommie and I admit that we don't pretend to be geniuses. You don't have to be a genius to be a successful teacher. That's what our book is about. Hope for all teachers. And what you can do to make success a reality for every student. But it helps if you are a bit crazy. Crazy enough to care more about children than you do about yourself. Take heart, though, if you are among the chosen who do care. Kingman Brewster Jr., a former Yale University president, was right when he said, "There is a correlation between the creative and the screwball. So we must suffer the screwball gladly."

Respect that.

Honor that.

About the Authors

Randall McCutcheon, nationally recognized by the Department of Education for innovation in curriculum, has authored eleven books, including *Can You Find It?*, a guide to teaching research skills to high school students, which received the 1990 Ben Franklin Award for best self-help book of the year; *Get Off My Brain*, a survival guide for students who hate to study, selected by the New York Public Library as one of 1998's Best Books for Teenagers; and three textbooks for speech and journalism courses. His most recent publications include a series of test-prep guides for the SAT and ACT: *Increase Your Score in 3 Minutes a Day: SAT Essay*; *Increase Your Score in 3 Minutes a Day: SAT Critical Reading*; *Increase Your Score in 3 Minutes a Day: ACT Essay*; and *Increase Your Score in 3 Minutes a Day: ACT Reading.*

After nearly a decade of working in radio and television, McCutcheon taught for twenty-seven years in both public and private schools in Iowa, Massachusetts, Nebraska, and New Mexico. He was selected State Teacher of the Year in Nebraska in 1985, and in 1987 he was named the National Forensic League National Coach of the Year. Elected to the National Forensic League Hall of Fame in 2001, he concluded a successful career as a high school speech and debate coach. In twenty-seven years, his speech teams won twenty-five state championships. More than two hundred of his students qualified to NFL Nationals, more than forty reached the semifinal rounds, twenty-five earned a place in the final round, and seven won national championships.

Tommie Lindsey has taught in public education for thirty years. After completing his undergraduate work at the University of San Francisco, Lindsey began his teaching career at Alameda County Juvenile Hall, moved to El Rancho Verde Alternative High School, and finally went on to establish the forensics program at James Logan High School (Union City, CA), where he has been its director for the past sixteen years.

The program at Logan received national recognition with the documentary *Accidental Hero: Room 408*, which won the Ashland Independent Film Award, the City Quest Film Award, and the Scine Golden Eagle Award. Several magazines have featured the program, including *People*, *Crisis*, and *Jet*. In 2002, the Logan Forensics Team was profiled on the "NewsHour with Jim Lehrer," and most recently Lindsey appeared on "The Oprah Winfrey Show" accepting a $100,000 Use Your Life Award for the team.

In 1994, Lindsey received the Smith College Omstead Award, which was given to four of the top teachers in the country for their innovation in education. Selected the California State Teacher of the Year in 1994, he was later elected to the California High School Speech Association Coaches Hall of Fame and was recognized by the National Forensic League as its National Coach of the Year. In 2002, Emory University presented Lindsey with the Pelham Award for his contribution to forensics and the community. Lindsey was honored as a MacArthur Foundation Fellow in 2004. In 2005, the Orange County Chapter of the organization 100 Black Men recognized him for excellence in education. Later that year, he was a "Bay Area Portraits: Everyday Acts of Courage" honoree for creating a better community environment.